Reigning In Righteousness

Regaining True Spiritual Authority By Fully Embracing Your Innocence!

Rudi Louw

Table of Contents

The Marvel of the Holy Bible

1. Uninterrupted Theme and Inspired Thought

It took *1,500 years* to compile the Holy Bible, involving *more than 40 different authors*. <u>Yet</u> the theme and inspired thought of Scripture continues *uninterrupted* from author to author, from beginning till end.

2. Absence of Mythical Stories

Compare philosophies and theories about creation in the Middle East, Europe, Asia, Africa, and Latin America and you'll find mythical scenarios: gods feuding and cutting up other gods to form the heavens and the earth, etc.

In ancient Greek mythology, Atlas carries the earth on his shoulders. In India, Hindus believe eight elephants carry the earth on their backs.

But in contrast, Job, the oldest book in the Holy Bible, declares that, *"God suspends the earth on nothing."* (Job 26:7)

This was said millennia before Isaac Newton discovered the invisible laws of gravity that delicately balance every planet and sun in its individual circuit.

In sharp contrast to every other ancient attempt to give a creation account, *the Holy Bible pictures the creation of the earth in a very scientific manner.*

For example: In Genesis Chapter One, the continents are lifted from the seas, then vegetation is formed and later animal life, all reproducing *'according to its own kind', **thus recognizing the fixed genetic laws.*** In addition, we have the bringing forth of man and woman, *all done by God in a dignified and proper manner, without mythological adornments.*

The balance or remainder of the Holy Bible follows suite.

*The narratives are **true historical documents**, faithfully reflecting society and culture **as history and archaeology would discover them thousands of years later. Not only is the Holy Bible historically accurate, it is also reliable when it deals with scientifically proven subjects.***

It was never intended to be a textbook on history, science, mathematics, or medicine. *However, when its writers touch on these subjects, **they often state facts that scientific advancement would not reveal, or*** *even consider, until thousands of years later.*

While many have doubted the accuracy of the Holy Bible, time and continued research have consistently demonstrated that the Word of God is better informed than its critics.

3. Intactness

Of all the ancient works of substantial size, *the Holy Bible survives intact, against all odds and expectations.*

Compared with other ancient writings, the Holy Bible has more manuscripts as evidence to support it than any ten pieces of classical literature combined!

The plays of William Shakespeare, for instance, were written about four hundred years ago, after the invention of the printing press. Many of his original writings and words have been lost in numerous sections, *yet the Holy Bible's uncanny preservation has weathered thousands of years of wars, contradictions, persecutions, fires and invasions.*

Through the centuries Jewish scribes have preserved the Holy Bible's Old Covenant text, **such as no other manuscripts have ever been preserved**. **They kept tabs on every letter, syllable, word and paragraph**. *They* *continued from generation to generation to appoint and train special groups of men within their culture* **whose sole duty it was to preserve and transmit these documents <u>with perfect accuracy and fidelity</u>**.

Who ever bothered to count the letters, syllables, or words of Plato, Aristotle, or Seneca for that matter?

When it comes to the New Testament, the actual number of preserved manuscripts is so great that it becomes overwhelming. *There are more than 5,680 Greek manuscripts, more than 10,000 Latin Vulgate manuscripts and at least 9,300 other versions. Further still, there exists an additional 25,000 manuscript copies of portions of the New Testament.* **No other document of antiquity even begins to approach such numbers.**

The closest in comparison is Homer's <u>Iliad</u>, with only 643 manuscripts. The first complete work of Homer only dates back to the 13th century.

4. Unmatched Accuracy in Predictive Foretelling

The Holy Bible is unmatched in accuracy in predictive foretelling. No other ancient work succeeds in this, or even begins to attempt this.

Other books such as the Koran, the Book of Mormon, and parts of the Veda claim divine inspiration; **but none of these books contain predictive foretelling.**

This one undeniable fact we know for certain: *While microscopic scrutiny would show up the imperfections, blemishes, and defects of any work of man, <u>it magnifies the beauties and perfection of God</u>. Just as every flower displays in accurate detail the reflection and perfection of beauty, <u>so does the Word of Truth when it is scrutinized</u>.*

Historian Philip Schaff wrote:

"Without money and weapons, Jesus the Christ conquered more millions than Alexander, Caesar, Muhammad, and Napoleon. Without science and learning, He (Jesus the Christ) shed more light on things human and divine than all philosophers and scholars combined. Without the eloquence of schools, He (Jesus the Christ) spoke such words of life as was never spoken before or since and produced effects which lie beyond the reach of orator or poet. Without writing a single line, He (Jesus the Christ) set more pens in motion and furnished themes for more sermons, orations, discussions, learned volumes, works of art, and songs of praise ***than the whole army of great men of ancient and modern times combined.****" (The Person of Christ, p33. 1913)*

Today, there are literally billions of Bibles in more than 2,000 languages.

Isn't it about time you find out what it really has to say?

Hey listen, the Holy Bible is all about Jesus, the Messiah, the Christ...

...and everything about Jesus Christ is really about YOU!!

Study Tips:

Read 2 Corinthians 5:14, 16, 18, 19, and 21.

In the light of these Scriptures, it should be obvious that, if you want to study the Holy Bible, *you should study it in the light of Mankind's redemption!*

Feed daily on **redemption realities** found in the book of Acts, in Romans Chapters One through Eight, and in Ephesians, Colossians, and Galatians. These realities are also found in 1 Peter Chapter One, 2 Peter Chapter One, James Chapter One, as well as in 1 and 2 Corinthians.

Foreword

Thank you for taking the time to read this book.

Let me start off by saying that *I am totally addicted to my Daddy's love for me.*

I am in love with Jesus Christ, *and that is enough for me!*

The love of God is so much more than a doctrine, a philosophy, or a theory. It is so much more and goes so much deeper than knowledge; *it way surpasses knowledge.* **We are talking heart language here.**

Thus, I write *to impact people's hearts,* to make them see the mysteries that have been hidden in Father God's heart concerning Christ Jesus, and actually *concerning THEM,* so as to arrest their conscience with it, *that I may introduce them to their original design and to their true selves,* **and present them to themselves perfect in Christ Jesus** *and set them apart unto Him **in love**,* as a chaste virgin.

We are involved with the biggest romance of the ages. Therefore this book cannot be read as you would a novel: *casually.* It is not a cleverly devised little myth or fable. **It contains revelation and *truth* into some things you may or may not have considered before.**

It is *the TRUTH of God, ultimate TRUTH, and therefore has direct bearing upon YOUR life.* The Word and the Spirit are my witness *to the reality of these things!*

Be like the people of Berea the apostle Paul ministered to in Acts 17:11. Open yourself up to study the revelation contained in this book *to discover for yourself the reality of these things*.

Be forewarned! Do not become guilty of the sins of the Pharisees, **or you too will miss out on the depth of fulfillment God Himself, who is LOVE, wants to give you**.

Jesus said of the Pharisees and Sadducees that they strain out every little gnat BUT swallow whole camels. What He meant by that is that *some people seem to have it all together when it comes to doctrine and they love to argue.* **It makes them feel important, but it is nothing other than EMPTY religious and intellectual pride.** *They know the Scriptures in and out, and YET they are still so IGNORANT about* **REAL TRUTH that is only found in LOVE.** They are always arguing over the use of *every little jot and tittle* and over the meaning and interpretation of **every word of Scripture,** *but they are still so ignorant and indifferent* **towards the things that REALLY MATTER!**

The exact thing they accuse everyone else of doing though, the precise thing they judge

12

everyone else for, *they are actually doing themselves.* That is **they often downright misinterpret and twist what is being said,** *making a big deal of insignificant things while obscuring or weakening God's real truth: the truth of His LOVE.* They are always majoring on minors **because they do not understand the heart of God and therefore they constantly miss the whole point of the message**.

Paul himself said it so beautifully,

*"...the letter kills but **the Spirit BRINGS LIFE;"***

*"...<u>knowledge puffs up</u>, but **LOVE EDIFIES**."*

I say again: *Allow yourself to get caught up in the revelation I am about to share.* Open yourself up to study the insight contained in this book, *not only with a desire to gain knowledge, but also with anticipation* **to hear from Father God yourself; to encounter Him through His Word, and to embrace truth, in order to know and believe the LOVE God has for <u>you</u>, and get so caught up in it, that you too may receive from Him LOVES' impartation of LIFE.**

The message proclaimed in the gospel and thus also revealed in this book is the voice and call of LOVE Himself to every human being on the face of this earth. *If you take heed to it, it is custom designed and guaranteed to forever alter and enrich your life!*

Acknowledgment

I want to acknowledge and thank one of my mentors in the faith, Francois du Toit, for blessing and impacting me with revelation knowledge.

I borrowed the portion on *"The Marvel of the Holy Bible"* from his website: http://www.MirrorWord.net, as students so often feel they have a right to do with things that come from teachers they respect. Just as Galatians 6:6 says, *"Let him who is taught the Word **share in all good things** with him who teaches."*

To all our dear friends and family, for all the love and support, and to all those who helped me with this project:

THANK YOU!

Also, especially to my wife, Carmen;

For keeping me real by being my companion in life and partner in ministry,

I love and appreciate you so very much!

"But the free gift is not like the trespass.

For if the many died, through the one Man (Adam's) trespass,

much more

have the grace of God and the free gift in the grace of the one man, Jesus Christ,

abounded for (the benefit of) (the same) many!

"...And **the free gift is not** like the effect

of that one Man (Adam's)
sin; **the free gift brings
righteousness!"**
"the gift of God's grace
through the one man,
Jesus Christ,
**has far more
powerfully effected**
mankind."
"God's act of grace
is **out of all proportion**
to Adam's wrong dong!"

"If, because of one Man
(Adam's) trespass,
death reigned
through that one Man,
much more
will those (the same many)
who have all received the
abundance of grace and the
free gift of righteousness
reign in life
through the one man,
Jesus Christ
(as a result of what He
revealed and accomplished,

and as a result of His
indwelling)!"
"For, if the **reign** of death
was **established**
by the one Man (Adam),
...**far more**
shall the **reign** of life
be **established**
in **all** those (**the same many**)
who have (mutually)
become the recipients of
the overflowing fullness
of the **free gift** of **righteousness**
<u>**by,**</u>

(and as a result of,
the reconciling work of)
the one man, Jesus Christ!"

"What shall we say then?
Are we to **continue** in sin
that grace may
(be forced to, or
have to continue to)
abound (even more)?

By no means! No way!
Not at all! God forbid!

(The point
beyond which one cannot go
has been reached.
There is **nothing else**
that God can possibly do,
to rescue us to the full,
from the Fall,
beyond what
He has already done
in Christ!)"

~ Romans 5:15-17
~ Romans 6:1

Prayer

Father we're so thankful for security in you!

We're so excited because of our prosperity in You!

We thank you precious Daddy God that You have made such large provision for us!

We thank you that we can testify today that we have become partakers of the abundant life!

We thank you that abundant life is ours!

…ours to enjoy,

…and ours to communicate!

Father, right now, we just ask that the Holy Spirit will speak to us in our hearts through the writing of this book!

We are hungry for You to speak to us, we don't want another mystery to confuse us; we want Your clarity,

…and we don't just want to hear another message to entertain our minds either Father,

…we mean business with You in our hearts!

Father I just want to open my heart to be ministered unto by the Holy Spirit, so that He may minister unto Your precious children in this book through me!

…So that the Holy Spirit will work within us to recognize Your ministry in our midst, precious Lord!

Holy Spirit we ask You to speak to us, to deal with us, to build into our spirit a capacity for God's presence,

…that You would renew us in our spirit, and bless us and strengthen us and anoint us in our inner-being, through revelation knowledge, and by Your mighty power!

…And Father, that You in Your goodness, through Your gospel truth will so enrich us and free us that we will walk in the liberty of it, even today already Lord, through this book!

…So that we can own our days; so that we can redeem our days, and take into possession the full potential of our day!

…I am talking about that potential to enjoy our inheritance in You, and to then lay a hold of and possess our full inheritance in this life!

Thank you that You have given our neighbors to us as an inheritance; the very ends of the earth as our inheritance to possess and enjoy!

Hallelujah!

Father, thank you that You have become our wisdom, that Jesus has become wisdom unto us, and that You teach us to make the most of every opportunity Lord!

Thank you for your anointing!

Thank you Holy Spirit that You reveal Jesus to us!

…That You reveal the heart of the Father to us!

…That You even reveal to us the deep things of the Heart of the Father as we seek them out!

Thank you that we are able to receive, *that we can indeed receive the deep things of God!*

…Thank you that by Your working within us we do not have the spirit of this world, but now instead we are thankful that we indeed have the Spirit who is from God, so that we might know the deep things of God; so that we may understand the things that have been bestowed upon us, and that have been freely given to us by God,

…Father, thank you that these things have been laid aside for all those who love You, to discover and richly enjoy!

So just rain upon our spirits from above!

Just rain Your truth within us!

Thank you Father that as the rain and snow come down from heaven, and water the earth, and do not return void, so shall Your word, so shall Your gospel be, and so shall Your truth and Your revelation be that You rain within us by Your Spirit, as we engage Your thoughts in this book, and encounter You through what You have to say in Christ Jesus, *the ultimate Word made flesh!*

Saturate us Lord, with Your truth, with revelation knowledge, with insight and understanding into the truth of the gospel, and therefore *with Your love and with Yourself!*

Father, we thank you that as Your truth finds its rightful place in our hearts and in our minds and in our lives, we thank you that we will indeed discover that the enemy has no more access to our minds to be able to direct us and influence us anymore!

…I thank you that even as people read this book, that Your revelation and Your truth will be so strong and clear that the enemy will not be able to interrupt or distract them with lack of concentration or interest, nor with lies.

Father thank you that through Your truth we have dominion over darkness, over all the forces of darkness and over all the power of the enemy!

Thank you Father that while we are receiving Your word *You are dispelling darkness!*

...and so, while we are embracing Your word, we together with You are dispelling the darkness from our lives,

...And we are being equipped, to use the truth, to dispel darkness from other people's lives as well!

Thank you Father!

Thank you that we may walk in covenant with You, in covenant agreement with Your truth, *and therefore in intimate covenant relationship with You,* because of it!

Thank you precious Father!

In Jesus name

Amen

Chapter 1

The Laws Of Identification!

I want us to study together in this book on the theme of *"the **Reign** of Righteousness"*

As we study the Scriptures together there are quite a few tremendous truths God wants us to discover, especially from the book of Romans, *concerning the **liberty** which the Laws of the Spirit; the Laws of Faith; the Laws of Appreciation **brings within us;** these perfect Laws of Liberty which **totally liberates us,** from the **dominion** of the Law of Sin and Death.*

That Law of the Spirit ...that Law of perfect liberty; the Spirit's laws, operates in the strength of *resurrection life!*

It is the resurrection of Jesus Christ that causes the Law of the Spirit; the Law of liberty; the Spirit's laws to operate, to be operative, to be powerful; *to be in powerful operation in our lives!*

*...Isn't it wonderful to discover God's Spirit to be **powerfully operative in our lives; through the Word of Truth; the gospel of our salvation!?*** It is, amen!

So now, I want us to go to the book of Romans, *because we want to fully understand the **reign** of righteousness,*

…So that our whole lives, and our whole ministry, and every aspect of our ministry, *will be a ministry of the **reign of righteousness**!*

That **righteousness** will release each and every one of us, in our lives and in our prayers, in our intercession for others, in our ministry, *to **dominate powerfully** over the enemy!*

So let's just quickly read a few Scriptures, just to warm ourselves up into this flow of thought,

…**So that we may be able to link up with the Holy Spirit, to junction with Him, and flow together with Him, in the liberty and in the power that He brings into us,**

…*And brings us into, amen!*

Thank you Holy Spirit!

Alright, go with me to Romans 5:12:

*"**Therefore, as Sin came into the world through one man, and Death through Sin, so death spread to all men, as all men sinned,** (or because all men sinned)."*

Let me just establish right off the bat that there was a law, the *Law of Identification* that began to operate with the sin of Adam …as far as our collective and personal interaction with the Fall is concerned.

Of course, there was and always has been *a greater Law of Identification already in operation,* as far as the spirit-dimension of our existence is concerned, according to Ephesians 1:4, and several other scriptures.

There is an association, an identification that existed between Christ and Man, *from way before the Fall even happened.*

So, it is actually in Christ, where that original Law of Identification originated …**and that is also therefore the very Law behind God's initiative in Creation, *as well as His initiative in our redemption and rescue.***

…But now, as far as the Fall is concerned, there is another Law of Identification that became activated, *affecting all of mankind with the sin of Adam.*

People often get stuck on that identification of us all in Adam, but you see, that other original greater Law of Identification in the spirit-realm was actually already in effect, before the sin and fall of Adam, **and remained in effect in spite of the sin and fall of Adam.**

You see, God identified Himself with Man, before creation, and therefore also in Creation, and thus, *God committed Himself to that original Law of Identification* when He created a body for us to live in, and then

31

brought Man forth in His own image after His own likeness, *from within Himself!*

God gave Man an automatic identity, when He said, *"Let us make Man: our image, our likeness!"*

…And thus you see, God committed Himself, to that original authentic Law of Identification!

A law is always something that operates, according to certain specific principles, and within certain rules and parameters.

…So, when a law is in operation, it is not just coincidence, amen!

The law of gravity is not just a coincidence, *it's a law, and it is operative!*

…And so it's there, and it operates, by pre-established principles, whether you recognize it, or not,

…Even whether you are aware of it, or not!

You see, you can even try and disregard the Law of gravity, and try and resist the Law of gravity, with your will, with sheer willpower, but eventually, no matter what you are trying to hold up in the air *with the power of your arm* …eventually, *the power of your will,* **will have to submit** to the Law or power of gravity, **because the power of your arm wears out.**

The power of your arm, your own strength, may seem like it is stronger, at first, *but later, gravity will have been proven to be stronger than the strength or power of your arm, **and the power of your will;*** it will eventually take its toll on you …because it is consistently operative and **it exercises its control over you; its dominion,** unbeknownst to you or not

…even whether you believe in it, or not!

So, that Law of Identification that came into operation in Adam and that has effected us all so powerfully, is a Law, *whether we believe in it, or not!*

…It's a Law, because it is an identification with, and an association with according to principle.

But, what I want you to see is that, even though this may be true, **even though we have come strongly under the influence of that Law of Identification, in Adam, *there is still, an even greater Identification that took place, in Christ, before time began, <u>an even stronger identification</u> by which we have all been identified.***

In Christ, in our association with Christ, God completely Identified Himself with all of mankind, in creation.

And so, that identification is greater than even our natural identification in Adam.

And you see, <u>that</u> original Law of Identification was <u>still</u> in existence, *and it was a greater and stronger Law,* than the Law of Identification that was put into operation in Adam!

God said, *"Man is created in My own image, after <u>our</u> own likeness."*

I want you to notice that the plurality of God was involved here, when God said, *"Let US make, (let Us bring forth) Man (from within ourselves); our image, our likeness,"* **and thus God gave Man an automatic identity, inseparable from theirs; It's <u>an unbreakable association and identification</u>!**

…an eternal <u>authentic</u> identity!

Amen, hallelujah!

Why did God give us an eternal authentic identity directly connected to His own?

Because, God wants to forever associate with and communicate with Man!

…God wants Man to be *His children!* Even more than that, God wants Man to be one with Him; *to be His bride, His companion in life – His life-long companion!*

When I was a boy, we went yearly on a month long vacation to Durban South Africa, embarking on the long 9 hour drive from Johannesburg or Klerksdorp, where we lived at

34

the time, all the way to Durban, or Amanzimtoti, just to be able to enjoy the ocean, and I still remember once coming back from one of our yearly vacations, with a parrot, named *"Kokkewiet."* We tried our best to get this parrot to become our friend, so that it would stop biting us, you know, because it had a sizable beak; a sharp one at that.

I therefore made it my job to communicate with this bird and try to get down to its level, you know, so we could befriend it.

So, I would speak funny, and try and get this bird to react, and be friendly, and communicate back. And so, eventually all our efforts paid off and we became good friends with the parrot and we essentially taught it to speak.

Actually, what I mean by that is, we taught it to repeat after us, or to say simple little sentences, when we trigger it's memory with a question or certain statement, *but it could not actually hold a multi-sentence conversation.*

The point I want to make is that you can get that parrot as friendly as you could possibly get a parrot to be. And you could even get it to do all kinds of tricks and stand on its head and do flips and all sorts of things and you can even get that parrot to talk, because they are marvelous creatures, **but you can never educate that parrot enough, in order to fully identify with it.**

Why is that?

Because, *a bird is a bird, and a Man is a Man!*

...We are not compatible!

...Because I am not of like-nature with it!

...It is not of the Man kind,

...And I am not of the bird kind.

So, the best you can hope for is that it can just be a good toy and a good pet,

...And it can offer some limited little bit of friendship and companionship,

...But that friendship and companionship would be inferior still,

And so, we could have some inferior level of relationship with that bird,

...But it could never fully satisfy my person,

...my being,

...Because there could never ever be any real identification,

...To the measure God intended association and identification to operate in.

You see God wants that automatic original association with us; His authentic Full Identification of us in Him, that shared identity, to be the very measure of our relationship with Him!

And you see, that automatic original authentic Identification we have all been identified with, that true identity, would then also be the foundation of our relationship and interaction *with one another.*

So, the implications of the fall of Adam, introducing Sin and the Fall and consequently some kind of a spiritual death to the human race, were that *our original deep identification and association with God, <u>as far as intimate relationship is concerned</u>, was now broken.*

That original Law of Identification and association was still in effect, *we were still children of God;* God still intimately knew *our true identity.* That didn't change ...*but as far as we were concerned, from our viewpoint, we lost our identity; our whole identity as children of God, and therefore also our intimate relationship with God, was broken ...it was destroyed!*

...*All because Sin was introduced,*

...*And the Fall came in,*

...*And then death came in,*

Death literally means: *a separation of some sort. ...A separation from life!*

Death came in; *some sort of separation from God came in, as far as us intimately relating to Him is concerned* ...*A separation from life* ...*from Life Himself* ... *A separation from God in intimate relationship came in.* Thus, we basically died *in our intimate relationship* with God. That's what happened.

We ceased to exist *as far as our fellowship and actual intimate relationship and friendship with God* is concerned,

...*All because of an illusion.*

...*All because a lie and a deception was introduced and embraced; it's called SIN,*

...*Sin came in;*

...*The Fall came in,*

...*And thus, "death came in, through Sin."* (Romans 5:12)

Do you see that?

Do you see how embracing the lie, the deception, how embracing SIN *introduced the illusion of separation,* and how that illusion became a ruling reality?

And so, its effect, the effect of Sin, the effect of the Fall, the effect of that illusion of separation, the effect of that death Adam began to experience and fully partake of

was that now every human being became identified with Sin, with that lie, that deception, that illusion of separation,

…And thus all of humanity came under the power of Sin; living by that lie, by that deception, by that illusion of separation.

How?

Through the Law of Identification; through that Law of our direct association with Adam as far as our natural origin is concerned!

When one man fell, *all men fell,* …*every person fell.*

And why is that? **Because *the initial lie, that deception* was transferred to the rest of us!**

Mankind became totally identified with fallen Man, *through Man's fall.*

Mankind became identified with Adam in his fall, *because of our immediate unavoidable close association with him, not as our spirit origin, but as far as our natural origin is concerrned.*

Why? Why can we say that? **Why can we say that the lie, the deception, the SIN *was transferred to the rest of us?***

Because of the legal immediate implications of Man's fall.

...Because you were identified and associated with Adam, in his fall.

...All because we were <u>in him</u>, literally, in his loins, when he fell.

So, as far as the Laws of the Universe is concerned; **as far as a strong governing principle,** *we all fell, when Adam fell.*

The Fall impacted us all *in a very real and practical way!*

Whatever happened to Adam, *at the same time, also happened to us!*

We were all identified in Adam; he fully represented the whole human race, *still unborn,* **...And, therefore, we were all identified with Sin, meaning,** *we all came under Sin's influence* **...we were made subject to Sin,**

...we came under the power of Sin, *and that death it introduced.*

You see, this is all because Adam's fall in the garden *had both legal and* **practical significance.**

It had practical significance, because it had legal significance.

But it also had legal significance, *because it had practical significance!*

You see, it was not just a matter between Adam and the Devil.

No, it was a matter between them, (Adam and Eve,) and the Devil, that's true, but …it also was a matter between them and the Devil, **and Adam's seed** …and also, therefore, between Adam and the Devil, **and the whole human race; <u>you and me included</u>!**

(Just as a side note here, do not get confused now okay. In these Scriptures out of Romans we are dealing with as a reference, Adam and Eve (Mankind) is referred to under one heading: ADAM. God sees Adam and Eve **as one unit; *they could not be separated,* and** that's why Paul constantly makes reference to them under one heading: **ADAM.**

He thus refers to **ADAM as a whole** and also then uses the phrase: *"...through the one Man, Adam,"* speaking about **the combined Adam** and how **that Adam** affected Mankind **as a whole** *and therefore individually as well*)

When God created Man in the garden, He created them male and female, *to be in His own image and in His own likeness.*

God created Man to be the seed, which would multiply and fill the earth, *with God's glory,*

*…**Because God's glory was in this man and in this woman.***

*But they fell, and the glory of God was
exposed, and became corrupted; as far as
their expression of that glory is concerned.*

*...Adam and Eve fell away from the glory of
God.*

For all practical intents and purposes *that
glory was lost to us;* it was lost <u>within</u>
Adam, it was lost <u>within</u> Eve; *they lost sight
of it, and therefore it was lost to us as well.*

*Adam and Eve, Mankind lost sight of the
glory of God within them when they
embraced the lie and death set in.*

*Thus, Adam as a whole, lost sight of the
glory of God within him ...and he lost his
consciousness of innocence ...when he
awakened to inferiority, and to shame, and
then to guilt.*

*When he awakened to SIN and to that
condemnation that comes with it; to the
consequences of it ...he then lost sight of
his innocence; he lost his consciousness
of innocence ...and thus death set in,*

*...and thus death spread to all men, through
the one Man, Adam.*

Romans 3:23 says,

*"Since all have sinned, and <u>fell</u> short of the
glory of God..." ...they fell <u>away from</u> the
glory of God*

*...In other words, **they all entered into a legal and practical relationship <u>with darkness</u> through this one Man, Adam.***

And thus, that DEATH, came into legal dominion, over Man.

That's why God said to Man, *"**You shall surely die!**"*

I want you to see that DEATH was not even considered, in the relationship that Man had with God, *before the Fall.*

God intended for Man, to be a partaker *of His eternal life,* **when He made Man.**

But DEATH, the very opposite of that eternal life, came in, and thus *the illusion of separation became <u>a ruling reality</u>!*

...And it all was solely a result of; it all was solely *the fruit of,* **Man's rebellion and his high treason;** *embracing the lie, embracing the deception.*

You see, the combined Adam committed high treason, when they sold out to the Devil, to the DIA+BOLOS – *to that influence that came into power through the introduction of Sin, which brought about the Fall.*

That's what the Devil's name means when you brake it down into its components. Devil is made up of the Greek words, DIA meaning,

through, and BOLOS, **to stumble, to be tripped up, to fall.**

...Thus the Devil's very name means: *That influence which came into dominion through the Fall.*

It all happened because Adam and Eve listened to the father of lies; to SATAN himself – to the SATANOS, *to the subtle voice of suspicion and accusation introduced in the garden; in the Fall ...that lying voice <u>that creates and sustains</u> the illusion of separation from God.*

I am referring to that subtle voice ...you know, the one that started off saying, *"Did God really say?"* ...that subtle lying voice that said:

*"God is lying to you about avoiding that other knowledge, because He knows that **in the day you eat of it, (in the day you partake of that other knowledge, other than the knowledge of God) your (spiritual) eyes will (finally) be opened and you will finally be like God** intimately knowing (and deciding) both good and evil for yourself."* - Genesis 3:1-5.

And you see, **we all swallowed that subtle accusation, *and that lie,*** hook, line, and sinker, and so, *the poisonous fruit of that tree, of that other knowledge* **is still in us to this day.**

You should really get my books, *"God's Love For You!"* and *"God's Inheritance In You!"* as well as the whole Study Course called: *"The Gospel in 3-D!"* to explore these concepts on Creation and the love of God for us some more, and these concepts I am sharing on this other tree, this other knowledge that was introduced to mankind in the Fall, *and how it effected and still affects **our righteousness and God's glory within us*** *to this very day.*

Reading those other books as well as that Study Course, in conjunction with this book, will really help you regain **the reign of righteousness** in your life!

But I am getting off track now. Can you see that there's a legal side to it all?

*…Otherwise the Law of Identification would not be true, **as far as our sins are concerned.***

The combined Adam (Adam and Eve), this one Man *died*; spiritually, practically speaking.

You see we need to establish this clearly, *that in* this one Man's death, **all *died*,**

…In order to also establish, how that, in Jesus Christ, in that one man's act of righteousness, *the same **all, was redeemed, and can now **all** enjoy salvation.***

The price for the restoration of faith, for the restoration of original authentic ultimate truth, *was and is sufficient!*

*"Through one Man's disobedience ...**so also,** through one man's obedience!"*

Can you see that **that** is the basis of the Law of Identification; *the very basis upon which it operates?*

That's why, the eternal Word, the Logos, God's original authentic blueprint Son, had to become the Christ, *the incarnate man, Jesus.*

The incarnation, is the very basis, for the Law of Identification in redemption.

God had to again, take upon Himself, the likeness of Man's being; *not his fallen being,* but his original blueprint being.

He had to become, a man, *the original ultimate Man!*

He had to take on, flesh and blood! *...He had to live, as a man, in this exact same body we live in! ...In order, to fully reveal, His original eternal identification with us ... to bring that greater Law of Identification into affect again ...and thus redeem the human body ...and redeem the original blueprint design of Man ...and so, to fully restore Man to his original glory ...to that very glory we lost in the garden ...that very glory within us, which we lost sight of and could no longer enjoy and give expression to!*

Jesus ultimately came to prove that separation from God is an illusion; *a convenient lie and deception we have all embraced and lived.*

He came to ultimately prove within himself – with the truth on open display in him; in His very person, *that our sin is merely the fruit of that illusion and deception, of that original lie we have all embraced and lived.*

...In the end, *because of what we see so clearly revealed in Him,* the lie did not *and will not* prevail.

Jesus came to put ultimate truth on display within himself, *in order to debunk and shatter the deception and illusion of separation from God!*

...*He came to defeat and destroy and undo the fruit of that original lie and deception we have all embraced!*

...*With an open statement of the truth He came to break the power of SIN and to ultimately restore us to our original design and to oneness with our Maker!*

...But I am now getting ahead of myself.

Chapter 2

The Legal Dominion Of Death!

You see, the dominion of death, *became a legal reality, a binding reality, a practical reality,* through Man's fall.

Let us just quickly look at Luke 4:6 in reference to that.

It talks about how the Devil came and tempted Jesus,

"...and the Devil said to Him, 'To You I will give all this authority and their glory...'"

(Remember, he showed Jesus all the kingdoms of His day in a moment of time.)

"'To You I will give all this authority and their glory, for it has been delivered to me, and I give it to whom I will'"

Now if Satan was lying there, *it would not be a valid temptation.*

I mean, it would not be a very real temptation to Jesus, amen.

If Satan was saying,

'…all this authority was given unto me,' …and yet it wasn't true …**then it wouldn't be a temptation,**

…but it was, a legal matter, <u>a ruling reality</u>, so that is why it was a valid, deliberate, very real temptation.

Do you see that?

Jesus came, for this very purpose. He came so that the kingdoms of this world and their glory *would indeed again become the kingdom of our God and of His Christ!*

…And you see, Satan knew it, Satan instinctively knew all this,

…But now Satan wanted Jesus *to take shortcuts.*

Satan was essentially saying,

'Jesus, don't go to the cross, or whatever it is Your Father told You to do, don't do it, I'll give You what You want, I'll just give it to You, let's organize a deal right now, You don't have to take the hard road and go through all kinds of suffering and whatever else that would be coming to You if You continue on this path of obeying Your Father and fulfilling His hearts desire, and to somehow try and take all this that I have gained from me, and take it for Yourself and for Your Father, listen, I'll give You all the kingdoms You want, I'll give You all this glory, I'll give You all its glory, for it was

50

once delivered to me, all You have to do to get it all is to take the easy way, without all that suffering and persecution that awaits You; just bow down to me and worship me!'

But of course, what Satan didn't realize is that Jesus did not come to try and negotiate with him, because you do not negotiate with a kidnapper and a terrorist; *you do not negotiate with a thief.*

No, Jesus came, as a man, not to gratify himself even; He came, as a man, and yet as God, **to win our hearts and minds** *by revealing the truth so clearly to us* **that it exposes Satan's lies and causes him to lose his authority over us.**

But, let's get back to our scripture there in Luke 4:6. When was all this glory, all Man's glory and authority, delivered to Satan?

In the very Garden of fellowship.

Satan came in, manipulated Man through lies and deception, and for all practical intents and purposes stole the glory of God!

He came and stole Man's glory; Man's authority!

And so, Man lost God's glory *…he lost that glory, because he lost his own glory in the garden, when he lost sight of the glory already within him, and fell away from it!*

...He lost his authority; the authority of truth, and therefore he lost that glory, that glory that God had given him!

...He lost sight of the glory of God within Him and the authority that comes with it!

"...all have sinned (...Man fell into sin **and lost the glory**) *...fallen short of the glory of God!"*

...And his authority went with it!

It was taken from him!

It was stolen!

So, when was all this glory and authority delivered to Satan?

In the beginning; *right there in the Garden.*

That's where SIN was embraced in fellowship; (that's where the high treason was committed,) *when the lie and deception came in and was introduced and embraced in full.*

All this glory and authority, was given to Man!

God gave Man, dominion!

God gave Man, the glory!

And Satan was after it!

And he sneaked into this thing, into this garden, into this garden of fellowship, and through deception; through lies and manipulation *he took it from Man, and it was delivered to him* – the very fellowship and glory and dominion of Man!

And so, by embracing the lie, Man came into fellowship with the Devil and under his influence and therefore under his dominion, legally.

So, before the cross of Jesus Christ, *Satan's dominion over Man was real,* through Man's embrace of Satan's lies and deception,

…And thus through Satan's very clever manipulation *it was a legal transaction and became legally binding – his influence, his dominion was now firmly established.*

I am writing from Man's perspective, from natural reality now, okay, *not from God's perspective now; not from eternal reality, okay.*

I go into more detail about **God's eternal perspective and God's eternal reality in spite of the Fall** in that Study Course, *"The Gospel In 3-D!"* I already mentioned, and then also in three of my other books, *"God's love for You!" "God's Eternal Purpose!"* and *"God's Inheritance in You!"* The book, *"You Are Totally Forgiven!"* should perhaps also be included in that.

But right now, I want to focus in, on this thing of the Fall.

I want to focus in on this thing of **Man losing the glory and authority that God gave him,**

…through one act, through one transgression, through one trespass.

…He lost it all, in a legal transaction with the Devil …it was a fellowship and an agreement that was entered into …a definite link, an association that was established, between Man, and Man's enemy, through manipulation; through lies and deception.

…Clearly Adam was in over his head in this conversation of confusion that became a legal transaction …this fellowship and agreement that was entered into with the SATANOS: the accuser and his false accusations and deception …the very Father Of Lies himself.

That's why we read in Ephesians that, the Devil, the DIABOLOS uses <u>this world</u> created through the Fall; this natural dimension of existence we have been reduced to and are stuck in; these false religious and social-political structures, we have inherited from our forefathers and been forced to be a part of, and reduced to live by, *to blind, the minds, of the unbelievers, from God …from the reality of*

God ...and from the truth of God ...from ultimate truth!

...And thus, he keeps them from enjoying intimate fellowship with God.

Ephesians 2:1 & 2 and 2 Corinthians 4:3 & 4 clearly says,

"...you were dead in your trespasses and sins, in which you once walked, following the course of this world,"

"...following, the prince, of the power, of the air, (that invisible influence inherited from our forefathers)*"*

"...that spirit, that is now at work, in the sons, of disobedience."

(Note: **They are still sons, *still children of God,*** but now they are the fruit, and bear the fruit, of disobedience; *of that initial disobedience.*)

Paul says,

"Even if our gospel is veiled, it is veiled only, to those, <u>who are perishing</u> (in their disobedience; their blindness, their deception)."

He says,

"In their case, the god of <u>this world</u>, (in other words: This world has become their

god, and the Devil uses it, and so it) has blinded, the minds, of the unbelievers."

Let's go back now to Romans 5:12. Paul says,

"Therefore, as Sin came into the world, and death through Sin, <u>thus death spread</u>, as all men sinned (or because all men sinned; having inherited that initial Sin from Adam and Eve)."

He says,

"Sin indeed was in the world, before the Law was given, but sin (which is merely the fruit of Sin) is not counted (or calculated accurately, for what it truly is; for what it leaves us with), where there is no Law,"

"…yet, death reigned,"

(…whether you know what you are missing out on or not, it is still happening to you! Thus, Sin, and its fruit of sin, whether it is counted or not, whether you think it counts or not, whether you know that thing is wrong or not; even if you don't know it, it is still wrong, and it is still having its affects upon you; including it's effects, the consequences of it, amen. *The main thing is that death reigned, whether we knew about it, or not.* **Thus that law of SIN and DEATH was in affect**.)

"…yet, death reigned, from Adam to Moses, even over those, whose sins, were not like, the transgression of Adam (Whether Adam's

56

*sin was the initial Sin, and our sins are merely the fruit of that Sin or not, doesn't matter; **it is all still the fruit of the same tree**)."*

*"...yet, **death reigned, from Adam to Moses, even over those, whose sins, were not like, the transgression of Adam** ...who was a type of the One who was to come."*

You see that Law of Identification, **set in,** the moment Adam sinned,

...and, **the implications** were ...*the* **result** of the Law of Identification was that,

...**Adam's sin was identified by Satan, *with every other person*** ...all because, **every other person's life, *was already identified with Adam*** ...*and so,* <u>mankind's fallen life, and mankind's sins</u>, can all be traced back to the fall of Adam.

So, the legal implications of the Law of Identification, were that, *death came into legal dominion,*

...death and sin came *into rule.*

...it came *into dominion!*

...and thus,

"...death <u>reigned!</u>"

But in all this, Adam was still only *"a <u>type</u> of the <u>One</u> who was to come:"*

...He still was only a copy of the original, and merely a prophetic picture and representation **of The Ultimate Source; the Son Himself; Jesus Christ –** *the ultimate Man; the authentic original blueprint of the human race!* - John 1:3-4, 9-10; Colossians 1:15-20.

Hopefully you are still following along with what I am saying.

I am trying not to complicate things too much, but to clarify them instead, so hang in there.

Chapter 3

Much More!

Okay now it says in verse 15, and I want you to clearly notice the distinction,

Romans 5:15,

*"__But__, **the free gift, is not like the trespass, for, if** (since) **many** (the many) **died, through the one Man's trespass, __much more__, have the grace of God, and the free gift, in the grace of that one man, Jesus Christ, abounded for** (the same) **many."***

Now listen to the Goodspeed Translation,

*"…**the free gift, have, __much more__ powerfully, affected mankind**"*

You see, we truly need to see this, and study this so we can get this!

I have been dwelling on this, and I tell you, my heart has been getting larger and larger in the understanding of this,

…because, I believe that if the Church of the Lord Jesus Christ ***can see*** *the full revelation of this truth, in fact, if our neighbors can see it too,* **we will all begin to walk in such**

authority and such dominion that *we will put the Devil to flight!*

Ha… ha… ha…

Hallelujah!

I mean, he will have to flee at such a speed,

…because we will be taking this nation, and the nations of the world, in short order, *just like that, ha... ha... ha...* **with such dominion and authority;** *with such liberating truth in what we speak* …and with such real spiritual power and authority, to undo his lies and deception, and his whole dominion, amen!

…And we'll do it, through truth and love …and with anointing and authority in our words and in our prayers, and in our laying on of hands.

…We'll do it with a clear understanding of the truth …and we would even hardly have to address the Devil, ha... ha... ha... but we will be dealing with him effectively, as we, by the anointing, **open people's eyes to this truth; *to the truth of their Daddy's love, and to the truth of their true design and identity in Him fully restored to them;* to the truth of their salvation, and to the truth of the gospel; to the truth of their successful redemption; their total restoration in Jesus Christ!**

I mean, all we would have to do is, awaken them, to *redemption realities,* and they

themselves will put the Devil to flight in their lives.

They will see the truth, *and be anointed by the truth,* and they will no longer yield to the Devil's lies, and to his deception, *and he will have nothing left; no ground to stand on!*

Listen, for many many centuries now, the Devil has had the Church *to believe the opposite;* **to believe that the Fall was the much more, *and the work of Jesus the much less!***

...To believe that he, the Devil, is the much more, *and we are, the much less!*

...And to believe that sin is the dominant issue! *...when in fact, sin is <u>not</u> the foremost issue!*

Correctly understanding and embracing the gospel; *the real truth of God, is the dominant issue!*

Grasping what God has to say about us, because of His eternal love dream, and because of what He has done and accomplished for us in redemption, that is the great issue, not sin, amen!

The Devil, for far too long, has had us all convinced that few and far between are the ones who are truly making it in life, you know, the guys who genuinely have something in the Spirit, and therefore making it as a Christian;

61

the spiritual giants, you know …**but hey listen, God made enough provision, through the gift of His Son,** *through the gift of righteousness,* **which absolutely, legally, and therefore, vitally, as a reality,** <u>*has already*</u> *affected mankind!*

And therefore, it can and <u>will</u>, far more powerfully, affect mankind, *through us,* **than what sin was ever able to do in affecting mankind.**

It is far more able, to affect mankind, than Sin was able to affect mankind!

What I'm saying to you is that, the gift of God's Son, *that gift of righteousness, will, far more powerfully affect mankind,* **than Sin was able to do through Adam** …*much more powerfully, than what Sin is able to do today, through the lie; through the Devil's deception!*

You see, that gift of righteousness, has *already been given to all men,* <u>**at the same time**</u> **as the gift of Christ was given to all men.**

Do you see that?

I also expound on this subject in one of my other books, *"Grace Exceedingly Sufficient,"* and you are welcome to get that and go read that one as well.

But hey listen, God has made provision through the gift of His Son, *through that gift of righteousness, which has far more powerfully affected mankind,* than what Sin affected mankind …*both, legally, and practically!*

Amen!? Hallelujah!

You see, legally, Adam's sin brought DEATH into dominion.

Legally, Adam's sin brought the DEVIL into dominion.

Legally, all the glory and the power and the authority of the kingdoms of this world, was delivered to the Devil.

And so, practically, vitally, Man became a slave!

For all practical intents and purposes he became an inferior being!

…And he had to hide his inferiority behind his pride!

Man became busy with his own efforts and works to try and become better; to try and change, but he became condemned, he became self-defeated, and he became subject to fear.

…He was subject to death; he was death doomed.

…He was subject to anxiety; he was subject to deception, and depression, *and all kinds of empty lusts and passions* …and he became self-destructive.

…He lived his life in self-destruct mode!

…He lived outside of his actual design, outside of his original design!

The vital, the practical result, of the legal reign of death over Man, *made a slave of Man.*

…And so, there he was, *a crippled being.*

…Created to be, and made, and brought forth, in the glory of God …*but now, crippled, under the dominion of ignorance and darkness!*

And so now, in order for him to even live, he has to live under self-delusion, *under the self-deception of pride.*

Why?

Because Man still wants to have some kind of dignity you see.

…He was created in dignity, and made for dignity; *for glory.*

…*So, Man keeps striving, and humanity is trying, to build himself up, through his finances and through his education.*

…Trying to find some kind of recognition.

…Trying to find acceptance …and to find that applause, you know, that he lost in the garden.

…But he remains under the dominion of death!

You can also go read about this in 3 of my other books, *"No Longer Looking for Applause!"; "God's Measure verses Man's Measure!"; and "Resurrection Life Now!"*

So, Man remains under the dominion of death …<u>but only until</u> faith is birthed and righteousness breaks through!

…<u>Only until</u> righteousness dawns on his spirit!

…<u>Only until</u> righteousness breaks that hold of death over Man, and that hold of Sin.

So, I like the translation that says that,

"…the gift of God's grace, has <u>far more powerfully</u> affected mankind."

…And how about this one,

"<u>Far greater</u>, is the gift, than was the transgression!"

…And notice also this one,

"God's act of grace, is <u>out of all proportion</u>, to Adam's wrongdoing!"

Ha... ha... ha... Hallelujah!

Can you see now, the basis, of this <u>much more</u> gospel; this <u>much-more</u>-ministry that we're involved with?

It makes you want to change the name of your ministry to, *"The Much More Ministries"*

Ha… ha… ha… Hallelujah!

You know at one time I was so stuck in legalistic thinking, and in a religious mentality, Old Testament ideas, and thought patterns, and ministry, that I wanted to call my ministry, *"Balaam's Ass Ministries!"* …because I always wanted to rebuke the sinners, and preach hell fire and brimstone to them, *until they repent!*

But, ha… ha… ha… God showed me, *"No way Jose"* …He showed me that Balaam's donkey had his mouth opened to speak, *not so he could join Balaam and rebuke the people alongside Balaam,* **but so he could rebuke the madness of the prophet!**

Ha... ha... ha... Ouch!

...Or is that, Oh me!

So, needless to say, now I would much rather prefer that name of, *"The Much More Ministries,"*

Ha… ha… ha… **because you see, we really are involved with the ministry,** (or the communication of something), *that is <u>much more powerful</u> in its affect; <u>in its potential</u>, than what sin or religion could ever be!*

Can you see that?

For years and years and years, we have been deceived in our religious ignorance, by the Devil himself, to think, *'Listen, you bunch of Christians, you are the weak ones. You are fighting a losing battle, and you might as well forget it, and just try and hang in there for dear life, until Jesus comes back to rescue his battered bride just in the nick of time, you know, before the antichrist spirit just completely takes over this globe, you know.*

…Oh, and God forbid you don't go up in the rapture, poor fellow, you are then going to have to make it through the terrible tribulation, and then finally, Jesus is going to get so mad, and so embarrassed, and with egg on His face He is going to have to come back on His white horse and save face, and pretend to be this victorious conqueror, you know.

…And He will personally now have to come and deal with that Devil yet again, you know, because the Church, God's crowning jewel, and Jesus' greatest achievement, was a failure, you see, because now they couldn't do it, you know …and, I mean this whole work of redemption was a complete and utter fiasco, a

failure, you see …Because God's whole experiment with Man proved to be a total disaster!'

No man, that is heresy; *it is deception for the Church to think like that!*

…To think that, '…you might as well Church, you might as well pray real hard that Heaven comes soon, and Jesus comes back quickly, to take you out of this mess …because Satan is going to take this world …Satan is just going to conquer this world, even the Christian world, because it belongs to him anyway!'

No! Nonsense!

Hey listen; the Bible says that *God <u>believes</u> in the gift of His Son …in that gift of righteousness!*

God *believes* there is *a lot more power* in the gift of His Son,

I mean, God *recognizes* that there is *a lot more power* in the gift of His Son, in the gift of righteousness, *and in the <u>affect</u> of that gift.*

…That gift is, *<u>out of all proportion</u>,*

…*The power in that gift is, <u>out of all proportion</u>,*

…*It is <u>out of all proportion</u> …You cannot even compare the two!*

68

It is <u>out of all proportion</u> to the power of sin ...*to the power of the enemy to keep Man bound!*

...It is <u>out of all proportion</u>!

And you see, *this is what He has invested in His Church!*

...It cannot even be compared!

Ha... ha... ha... **You cannot even compare the two!**

We are seated with Christ in heavenly places, in that unseen realm of spirit reality ...*in a place of authority ...far above ...not just above ...no, <u>far above</u> ...<u>all</u> rule and authority ...<u>every</u> principality, and <u>every</u> power, and authority and dominion ...<u>every</u> name and <u>every</u> powerful influence that can even be named ...in this age ...or even in all the future ages that haven't come yet.*

...*All because we are seated there with Jesus ...we are seated with Him ...in that realm of authority ...through that gift of Christ ...through that gift of righteousness! ...through that <u>full restoration</u> of everything we lost; everything the Devil took from us, there in that Garden.*

...We are seated with Jesus, in that unseen realm, in that spirit-realm, in that realm of spiritual authority ...*through the gift*

...through the restoration of that glory we lost.

Oh yes, in Jesus Christ and His redemption and reconciling work, *we are <u>fully</u> restored to that glory; to our original and authentic identity as children of God, and therefore to that place of freedom and life and dominion!*

...And yet, here we are and we're still busy with inferior thoughts; we're still thinking,

'Oh Adam sinned, and oh Lord, ugh Adam, brother, you've blown it, you've totally blown it for the rest of us, man, you've blown it. Just look at the mess you've brought us into. It's a total mess you've brought us into!'

...And so you see, we've *abided* in Adam, instead of Christ!

...And we've *idolized* Adam, and feeling bad about his fall, and exalting his fall.

...But hey no, listen, *in God's heart, in God's thought, in God's reality, what God knows to be the truth, what God knows to be a greater reality* ...*in God's grace,* Jesus did something *of a far greater reality;* He did something *far greater* than what Adam could ever have done!

Hey listen; in that grace, in that sacrifice, *in the present tense,* Jesus did something, <u>much greater</u>! ...*Much more powerful!*

...And that's why Paul said, *"...**much more powerfully, will the gift of His grace, affect mankind!**"*

That's what God has to say about the matter!

And listen, if we genuinely believe this, *if you truly believe this, if we honestly get the revelation of this,* I'm telling you, we are not going to bow the knee to any circumstance, to any deception, any more!

...And we are not going to bow the knee to any resistance either; to any attempt of the enemy, any attempt of the Devil, *to intimidate us.*

And why is that?

*...**Because we finally realize that his legal hold over mankind <u>has been broken</u>!***

The only hold that Satan maintains now, is through *deception!*

It's his <u>only</u> power!

...It's his <u>only</u> ability!

...It's his <u>only</u> hold.

I repeat again: **The <u>only</u> ability that the Devil can operate in *is through deception.***

He is nothing but the father of lies!

...But I am telling you now that, <u>the truth</u> *is much more powerful* than the lie!

Let's believe that!

Let's believe the truth of the gospel!

We'll better believe it, *or we'll never get anywhere!*

...I am telling you, *unless we truly believe the amazing truth* revealed in Jesus and in the gospel, *we'll never be able to reign!*

Chapter 4

The Humanity And Ministry Of Jesus Christ!

I want us to clearly understand that Jesus, while He was on earth as a man, in His ministry, *He operated in the very authority He was about to deliver to His Church!*

Jesus came to demonstrate that reign of righteousness.

You see, we need to understand that in the incarnation, Jesus, first of all, became identified with Man, *with the original and true design of Man.*

…**He became identified with Adam, as he was before the Fall,** *and not in his fallen state.*

…**He did not become identified with Man** *in Man's fallen state,*

He became identified with Adam, as he was before the Fall, *and not in his fallen state; not in that nature of Sin and death,*

Jesus did not submit to that bondage under that Law of Sin and Death …because then, He also would have been a sinner …and He would have had to be subject himself, to Sin and its nature.

...But you see, according to Hebrews 2:14,

He came, and He identified with Man; *with the image and likeness of God in Man* ...*by partaking of flesh and blood.*

It was only **on the cross that He identified himself with the curse,** *and absorbed the entire curse!*

On the cross, He became Sin for us!

On the cross, He represented that whole thing that separated Man from God!

On the cross, He represented that Law of Sin and Death!

On the cross, He became Sin for us!

On the cross, He represented the Fall in its totality ...*and He* <u>*identified*</u> *fully, with that curse, and became Sin for us,* **and thus prophetically cried out with us; with the cry of deceived, and confused, fallen Man,** *"My God, My God, why have you forsaken me!?"* - Matthew 27:46; Psalm 22:1.

But I want you to know that at no time was the Son ever separated from the Father; *They are one!* **You cannot separate the Godhead. There is no separation in the Godhead. The fullness of the Godhead was**

represented within Christ! It was the entire Godhead, Father, Son, and Spirit that was personally present in the man, Jesus Christ, *reconciling a wayward world back to Them.*

...So, Jesus fully associated with us in our feelings of abandonment; *He fully represented the human race,* and in the utterance of that cry **coming form fallen humanity,** *"My God, My God, why have you forsaken me,"* **God, within Jesus, answered our cry** ...*Emmanuel, God with us, God in us, answered our cry,* and by everything He was doing, even in the silent demonstration of His immense love for humanity, He came to say: *"I have not abandoned you; you are not separated form Me; I have never been separated form you! I have never stopped loving you! That separation and those feelings of abandonment is a lie and an illusion, a deception I have come to debunk and obliterate in my love! In all that I am doing and demonstrating to you now, this is my message to you: 'You stand totally forgiven and fully embraced, because you are loved immensely!'"*

...*You see, Jesus did not become separated form God, with our separation, because that separation was a lie and an illusion; the fruit of deception, to begin with.*

He came to tear down every wall of division and to remove every obstacle, every mountain was brought low, every low place was filled up and leveled out, even the rough places was made smooth, *in order to establish an unhindered uninterrupted connection in friendship and fellowship and romance and intimacy again.*

He came to destroy the works of our enemy; the Devil!

He came in person in order to break down every stronghold within our minds!

He came in order to do away with every wall of division!

He came to do away with the idea of separation!

He took on that whole death thing; that whole sin and separation thing; that entire lie ...in order to do away with it altogether and prove His unfailing love for us, to us.

I love the fact that Psalm 22:24 affirms that, *"He* (God the Father) *has not hidden His face from Him* (Jesus)*!"*

...Even when Jesus fully represented SIN in all it's ugliness on that cross, *the Father did not turn His face from Him!*

Hey this is huge! The Father has never turned His face from the Son, *nor has He ever turned His face from us!*

It is a lie that the Father could no longer look at His own Son, *because He became equal to Sin, and fully represented Sin on that cross.*

It is also a lie that the Son died, *spiritually speaking!*

No, on the contrary, He did not accepted the curse of Man's separation from God, upon Himself, *because that curse, that separation was a lie to begin with!*

Jesus removed every idea of separation; He removed every idea of God's wrath, and of punishment that was due us!

...Because God never intended separation, wrath, or punishment for us!

John makes it plain in John 5:22-23 when he quotes Jesus himself and says,

"The Father judges no one, but has given all judgment to the Son, so that through the Son all may honor and glorify the Father (for who He really is), and also honor the Son, as they honor the Father. Whoever does not recognize the Son and honor Him for what He came to reveal and do, does not honor the Father either who sent Him."

So, the Father judges no one, *but instead gave all judgment to the Son* to do something about it and deal with it and do away with it.

Thus, Jesus took the total curse of Man's fall *and supposed punishment due him, upon Himself, <u>and He personally absorbed it all, and dissolved it all</u>!*

He took the full blow of that idea of wrath *that we were cursed with, by the Devil and by our wrongdoing and transgression ...In His sufferings on the cross He fully absorbed that lie, that supposed wrath of God that Man was cursed with, to expect and anticipate, and that was now supposedly Man's due, <u>and He dissolved it</u>!*

...*He drew all judgment to Himself ...and in His death He dissolved it!* - John 12:27-33.

...*And with it He totally cast out all fear; He dissolved the fear of punishment!*

I say again: *In His death; <u>in the demonstration of God's perfect love for us</u>, Jesus did away with any idea of separation from God, and at the same time also, did away with all fear that has to do with punishment!*

In perfect love there is no room for terror!

...And I know this may be a bit of a rabbit trail, but I just feel the need to share this with you too:

If we look at the word "discipline" for instance, in the Bible the word "discipline" literally means: **to train.**

Discipline involves the necessary instructions, guidance, and occasional correction which helps provide someone the proper direction they need in order to succeed.

Thus, it is no wonder that the words, "**disciple**" and "**discipline**" share the same root, and is so closely related that the two words are even alike in application, for a disciple is indeed "disciplined" / "**trained**" by a teacher more wise and experienced than them.

...And let me tell you that God our Father, **through the Holy Spirit of truth,** is the ultimate teacher, *unveiling to us the mysteries of the universe; the very mysteries of both God and Man revealed **in the person of Jesus Christ!***

Unfortunately in our modern day and age the word, "discipline" is often seen in a negative light, in fact, so much so that in a typical disciple and teacher scenario, the instruction given by a teacher is regulated through the threat of punishment and then also followed up with said punishment, if the instruction given is not followed or fulfilled to a T. Thus the words, "discipline" and "punishment" have, in most people's minds, melted together into one and is seen as the same thing, *when it should most certainly not be the case.*

It was never meant to be seen as the same thing, *especially if you begin to contemplate the kind of enlightenment Jesus had in mind for us in discipleship,* **through the Spirit of wisdom and revelation in the knowledge of Him.**

You see, "discipline" and "punishment" are really two **vastly different realities.** They are two **separate,** *totally unrelated concepts* **altogether.**

Discipline has nothing to do with punishment!

Jesus didn't ever punish His disciples!

...He may have sternly rebuked and corrected them at times when they entertained inferior, negative, and restrictive mindsets, *but He never punished them for their mistakes or wayward thinking* ...**not even when one of them hacked off the ear of another man, or openly betrayed Jesus in public three times,** *because of misguided thoughts and miss-placed fears.*

You see, while discipline's aim is to lead someone into a better way of thinking and a better life because of it, filled with good things, **through training them in the way they should think and go,** punishment's aim on the other hand, is giving someone *what they deserve for their wrong actions.*

Can you see that these two concepts are vastly different from each other?

Punishment is derived from the nature of the law; *It has nothing to do with discipline, but everything to do with fear, or terror.*

While LOVE on the other hand, God Himself, *drives out all fear ...and even the need for punishment!*

Therefore, it is not just a small thing, but a dramatically big mistake to confuse the word, "discipline" with "punishment" and to see them as the same thing.

God is so adamantly opposed to both *fear and punishment* **that that is exactly what He came in person to demonstrate in Jesus Christ.**

I think it is in Hebrews 12:5-6 where us Christians get some of our confusion from in the New Testament, when it comes to seeing discipline and punishment as the same thing, *for it is mentioned in the same breath, or in the same sentence there.*

...And yet, Hebrews 12:5-6 is a direct quote out of Proverbs 3:11-12, *but it is a miss-quote you see.*

I strongly believe that the last part of those verses in Hebrews 12:5-6 were tampered with by someone other than the original author of this letter to the Hebrews, *to end up saying something that was never said, or meant to be said, by the original author.*

So whether it was the original author's own words, *because of some remaining law-oriented wrong thinking,* or whether the text was tampered with, either way, **it does not line up with the original quote out of Proverbs 3:11-12,** *which is worded much better, and much more accurately reflects the heart of God for us,* (which is in essence what was revealed in Jesus, and what this whole letter to the Hebrews was supposed to be all about).

Hebrews 12:5-6 reads:

"My son, do not make light of the Lord's discipline (the author of Hebrews is quoting out of Proverbs 3:11-12, but is talking about the Lord's **instruction to us, *found in His ultimate Word to us, made flesh*** in Jesus Christ), *and do not lose heart when He sternly rebukes you,* (through the truth of redemption; through this ultimate Word and instruction to you, made flesh in Jesus Christ, **because your thinking is wrong**) *for remember that the Lord disciplines those He loves..."*

...And here comes the added (or tampered with piece):

*"...And He **punishes** everyone He accepts as a son."*

The original verse this scripture was directly quoted from, in Proverbs 3:11-12, does not have that last bit in it at all.

It reads instead:

"My son, do not make light of the Lord's discipline, and do not lose heart when He sternly rebukes you, (Just like Jesus often did with the Pharisees, **because of their warped thinking**), *because the Lord disciplines those He loves..."*

...Note that up to now the quote is almost word for word the same, and accurate, but now notice also how different it reads in this last part. I says:

*"...He disciplines those He loves ...**as a father the son he delights in.**"*

You see, God is a good God, One who *"delights in His children."*

He is not some kind of "ogre," as this sudden change in scripture tends to suggest, and wants us to think.

Now the word, **"punishment"** does not even just suggest a mere light spanking from a loving daddy, which is a bad enough idea; *a contradictory idea in and of itself,* but no, it even suggests something much worse. The word, "punishment" speaks of **a full-blown thrashing which leaves one bloody and near death!**

Listen, I say again: Whenever the word, "punishment" is used **it describes exactly what the Sanhedrin and Roman government**

did to Jesus. Whenever the word, "punishment" is used, it is used **in conjunction with scourging, and chastisement of the worse kind, akin to the bloody thrashing of punishment dealt out to Jesus by both the Jewish Sanhedrin and Roman authorities, and which Jesus had to endure, by the hands of evil men, the entire night before and then ultimately when they nailed Him to the cross,** just so that when we were at our worst, manifesting our wort evil against Deity yet, the God **who is love** could, *in contrast to all that,* **demonstrate His nature, and His immense love for us, to us, which revealed our enormous value and worth to Him, as well as the fact that we are His own dear children, whom He loves with a passion;** *the very passion of Christ.*

That is why John then also says in one of his letters to us:

"Love is perfected within us through the thought, through the knowing that as He is, so are we, in this world (talking about Jesus). In other words: We are all children of God, and that thought, that knowing enables us to face any judgment and condemnation coming from Satan, from ourselves, or from others, with confidence, in fact we can face any size crisis we are challenged with in our day to day living, with confidence!

And why is that?

Because God's perfect love for us revealed to us in Jesus casts out all fear; even the belief that has to do with any kind of punishment.

Hey, THERE IS NO FEAR in love.

I love the way John clarifies for us in 1 John 4:18 the difference between "discipline" and "punishment." **He places the two concepts in direct conflict with each other; as diametrically apposed to each other, *with love as the thing that wins out over "judgment" and "punishment,"*** and therefore essentially and effectively ending the debate of: "discipline" versus "punishment."

Listen again to what he says; he emphatically states that,

"There is no fear in love; (no room for terror or dread of any kind), *but* (instead) *God's perfect love* (for us, in fact) *drives out,* (or casts out), *ALL FEAR, **because fear has to do with torment associated with punishment,*** (and therefore in His immense love for us He Himself took both punishment and the fear of it out of the equation)."

He clearly tells us in verse 17 why He did that:

*"...Because, as He is, **so are we,** (even) in this world."*

In other words: ***We are His very own dear children, whom He passionately loves, even***

immensely so, *just as a father loves his* children **whom he delights in.**

Hey, *"God is LOVE."*

...**And in His love for us, He casts out all fear that comes from a belief in some sort of punishment due** *and still yet to come.*

Listen; neither "fear" not "thoughts of severe punishment" has any place in an intimate relationship with a loving God!

...**Just like there is no place for "fear" of any kind, and especially "the fear of harm," in an intimate love relationship between a husband and wife.**

You see, genuine love will always drive out fear!

...And why is that?

Hey listen, genuine love will always cast out all fear, *because fear will ruin intimacy, trust, and romance.*

Any husband who genuinely loves his wife will always drive away and cast out any thoughts of fear towards him that might exist in his wife's heart.

So, there are these two opposing and opposite forces of the universe, set forth here in 1 John 4:17-19, which are plainly set at odds against each other, *just like light and darkness.* The two forces set against each other as John describes them are: "Fear, which comes from thoughts and beliefs related to the idea of punishment," **versus** "Love, the kind of love, perfect love, which is directly introduced to us, by God Himself, in the person of Jesus Christ."

John goes on to say:

"Those who are still tormented by fear, any kind of fear, even the fear of some kind of punishment in the now, or judgment still to come somewhere down the road, (<u>has ignored the judgment Jesus already faced</u>) and have not been made perfect in (their comprehension of God's perfect) love yet!"

So, take your pick: You can believe that God wants to show His love to you, **by sometimes beating you severely even,** just like what was done to Jesus by actual hateful people. But, ha... ha.. ha... no man, that's not love!

...Or you can believe instead that your Daddy TRULY loves you, and wants to demonstrate that great love for you, to you *"by delighting in you"* and discipling you and disciplining / **training** you through the ultimate Word of Truth; the truth of redemption – the gospel of you being fully restored, by being totally redeemed **and revealed as <u>complete</u>** in Christ Jesus.

"Hey, we are saturated with and sustained by His love, through the truth that <u>He first loved us</u>!"

Let me tell you the honest truth about me, and that is that **the knowledge of God's delight in me governs my moral life *much better than the fear of punishment ever has or ever will.***

Someone might be wondering: But what about *"the fear of the Lord?"*

Ha... ha... ha... I am so glad you asked,

Hey listen, *"the fear of the Lord **is the beginning of wisdom."*** (Proverbs 9:10), and so that *"fear of the Lord,"* **is a wonderful thing!**

You see, the fear of the Lord is the exact opposite thing, the antidote, to the fear (or terror) of punishment.

The fear of the Lord is quite possibly one of the most exhilarating and liberating experiences and revelations you could ever have!

Where the Spirit of the Lord is present; where the Spirit of the Lord is, there is liberty; absolute liberty – no fear there!

In fact, in His presence, there is fullness of joy!

You see, the fear of the Lord is so vastly different from any other kind of fear (dread, or terror) mentioned in Scripture.

When talking about the holiness of God, or "the fear of the Lord," the word, REVERENCE comes to mind, and yet, even that word, "reverence" becomes a total understatement when someone experiences the very "fear of the Lord," or the very person of God for themselves.

It is an important and often overlooked fact that the word for "fear," as in *"the FEAR of the Lord,"* in the Hebrew language primarily refers to the concept of AWE.

Religion has tried to convince us otherwise; religion has tried to convince us that it means something else, *when it doesn't!*

...They have tried to introduce "GOD" and "TERROR" to us in the same sentence, *when the two do not belong together and has nothing in common.*

Please comprehend that in the person of Jesus Christ, God Himself makes it abundantly clear that the fear of the Lord has nothing to do with fearing that you will somehow be destroyed by this God of holiness, if you even dare to approach Him.

In Jesus Christ, God Himself reveals in person that the fear of the Lord has everything to do with *being totally overcome and overwhelmed by His foreign to us, exceedingly, out of this world, goodness!*

He, God the Father, who finally revealed Himself in His immense and intense love, in person, in EMANUAL, in the person of Jesus Christ, is unlike anything or anyone that we have ever encountered.

Let me say that again: **The entire GODHEAD whom we worship as GOD, in their very being; in their immense and intense LOVE is unlike anything or anyone that we have ever encountered.**

God our Father, revealed in the entire Godhead, Father, Son, and Spirit is set apart in the immenseness of His love and goodness, or He is "holy" if you will, in the greatness of His love and goodness, *in a way that is so unfamiliar to us, and yet so totally disarming*, because you see, He in His holiness, He in the very purity of love, *is the total fulfillment of the desire of our hearts.*

You see, that is exactly why the fear of the Lord drives out all fear!

We tremble in His presence, not in fear, but we tremble because of His overwhelming goodness!

...Just as Hosea 3:5 declares that, *"In the last days, they will tremble in awe of the Lord and His goodness!"*

The only way God and terror can possibly be mentioned together in the same sentence is either when He who is love drives it out, or when we see His beauty, for when we see Him in His beauty, that beauty, that "holiness" then works on us to overwhelm us, just like terror used to undo us and take us over.

So, the fear of the Lord alive in our hearts looks more like the adoration and worship we freely give to God for His beauty, and because of the impact of His immense love for us upon our hearts, than it looks like dread that God is going to squash us like a bug for sins we may have committed against Him.

In fact, the fear of the Lord cannot be something that involves ANY feelings of fear or dread towards God.

...And why do I say that?

Because, the truth is, when you become AWED by Him in His full beauty; when you become AWED by Him in His love; when you become AWED by Him in His holiness, when you become AWED by Him in the work of redemption, *it would be a total insult to that LOVE DEMONSTRATED, to still hold on to ANY fear, dread, or terror!*

That is John's point in 1 John 4:18. **If we still continue to feel fear towards God, rather than AWE, in the light of His immense love for us demonstrated, *it is an unfounded fear,* and it should then be a clear indication** to us that something is off or amiss in our understanding, and we do not grasp His PERFECT LOVE yet.

So, an inaccurate or incomplete understanding would be THE ONLY REASON **why there is something wrong with our love for God;** *why it isn't quite coming alive like it should.*

Listen; His PERFECT LOVE comes to us without threats!

Do not allow anyone to tell you that your deep-seated fears towards God, inherited from your forefathers, whether subtle or overt *are a good thing.* **It is not!**

It results in our love being hindered towards God, *rather than promoted,* **and it stunts and halts an intimate love-relationship with Him,** *rather than growing our love for Him to its full capacity.*

The reality is that as long as you still believe that God only tolerates you because of Jesus, and barely at that, and that He is still mad at you over something, and can hardly stand to be around you, and that He wants to, and is going to, punish you for something, in the here and now, *or even in the not so near and distant future* **...as long as you are holding on to those beliefs,** *the inevitable result will be that you won't want to, or be able to, get close to God, or close enough anyway, <u>to enjoy real romance and true intimacy with Him</u>.*

92

True vulnerability *only works when you BELIEVE you are COMPLETELY INNOCENT.*

You see, an opening of the heart to intimacy, real intimacy, deep intimacy, *can only take place in the context of trust and safety!*

I say again: **If you still believe the Lord will afflict you with some sort of "punishment" either in the now, or in the future somewhere,** *you will miss out on genuine deep intimacy.*

Genuine deep intimacy and romance only flourishes in an environment of perfect love!

Still fearing God's "punishment" is ALWAYS an indication of immaturity in the life of the believer, and it inevitably shows their need *to more fully comprehend the length and breadth and depth and height of His love, so that they may finally feel SAFE in God's presence, and begin to BE FILLED with all THE LOVE AND FULLNESS of God.*

I am so glad we are not somehow hidden in Christ *from God,* no, Jesus came to reveal that we are hidden with Christ *in God.*

He came to restore us to that reality; to that place in Him, *within the Father's bosom!*

He came to reveal that God's most immediate nearness, and our constant oneness with Him, *is indeed our portion!*

Intimacy with God is our portion; *our constant!*

Hey, God knows you, better than you even know yourself, after all He designed you and brought you forth *from within Himself!*

God intimately knows you, *and He loves what He knows about you!* His word of truth *defines you best!*

You are not merely the product of your parent's desires, no you are God's greatest idea, come to life, and you are every bit as distinctly unique as your fingerprint. You are indeed *very special and very dear to God!* You are His one of a kind masterpiece! *The masterpiece of His heart!* He not only loves you *immensely,* but He *likes you.*

He brought you forth *from within Himself; from within His heart* and He placed you in your mother's womb *as His offspring,* and there He clothed you with flesh.

Hey, you are so much more than flesh! God is your true origin; not your mother's womb, *and He desires you!* He wants *you!* He wants *you* to share in and enjoy the abundance of His love for *you.* He wants to romance *you!* He doesn't even want to use

94

you; *He simply wants to love you!* (Religion has made a big deal of their fear mongering message, and of their false motivation, saying that God can and *might* even use you, *if you measure up!*); But hey, there are no hoops to jump through; *He simply loves you!*

Everything we now are, and do, as a Christian, gets birthed out of that revelation that *He simply wants to love me and you!*

That is exactly why Jesus drew all judgment to Himself, every false concept of God's wrath, *the whole of it that was supposedly due Man,* according to religion, and ultimately according to Satan, the accuser of the brethren; the father of lies himself ...Jesus drew it all to himself, that entire lie of inevitable judgment due; *all the judgment supposedly due Man,* He drew it all to Himself, all judgment, and took it all upon Himself, and He took it down to the grave with Him, where it belongs, ... *because we were never meant for it!*

I say again: **God is love! God is our Father!** ...And **_the Father judges no one_**! - John 5:22.

You should really get my book, *"You Are Totally Forgiven!"* if you want to look deeper into and study more closely these amazing liberating concepts of Jesus revealing the Father's heart **by absorbing all judgment, taking it down to the grave with him, and** thus *removing it completely out of the equation.*

Hey, sin did not create grace!

Sin is not the gravity that grace orbits!

The Father, Son and Spirit communing around other centered love in Their intimate union from way before creation; *that fullness* is where grace originates and what it's all about!

In Jesus the entire Godhead came to demonstrate that grace, *and to invite us into it.* We are invited into that same Divine fellowship; *into Their same enjoyment of <u>fullness</u>.*

The entire Godhead has invited us into Their same enjoyment; *to come and enjoy other centered love within Their embrace!*

Hey, Jesus came to change the worthless conversation within ourselves about ourselves and others *to one that celebrates our true origin, worth and value!*

Isn't it wonderful to discover that what we have been invited into *is the greatest celebration of the ages!?*

...Because, in Jesus Christ, the God of mercy, who is in very nature MERCY; *the One who is MERCY personified, <u>forever triumphed</u>* ...<u>over judgment</u>!

"The <u>steadfast love</u> of the Lord never ceases; <u>His mercies never come to an end;</u> they are new every morning; <u>great is His faithfulness</u>!" - Lamentations 3:22-36.

Father God came in person, to rescue us from the inferior, futile, worthless ways and religious beliefs we inherited from our forefathers, *<u>by revealing to us our eternal value to Him</u>,* in the precious blood of Jesus Christ, *<u>both demonstrating and declaring</u>* through the lengths He was prepared to go to, and the price He was prepared to pay, that *He would rather die than live without us!*

...Thus, the very thing that makes the blood of Jesus so exceedingly precious is not that it was some form of pay-off to the Devil, or some form of payment for sin, but what makes it so exceedingly precious is <u>its message</u>; its value is in what <u>it says</u> to you and me!

Oh yes, God came in person and spoke the inferior law language and scapegoat language of the Jews; He came and spoke the inferior religious judgment-language of all Mankind – He came and spoke the inferior language of lambs, and sacrifices due, and of payment made, and judgment avoided or averted, *only to bring an end to that language.* He came to subvert our inferior religious judgment-language *with a message of His own, a higher language, the language of love; the greater message of our eternal value and worth!*

It really is the most amazing thing to discover that **our Father who knew us individually, completely, long before He formed us, *is the same Engineer who knew every minute detail of our being as we grew mystically in the secret sanctuary of our mother's womb! And knows us now, and longs to introduce us to ourselves again, so that we may know, even as we have always been known!*** - Jeremiah 1:5; 1 Corinthians 13:12.

So, *in light of all that; **in view of all this wonderful revelation I have just shared,*** people often ask me: *'So, what do you do about the reality of Hell then; what do you believe about it?'* If you want to know what I believe about Hell, I do not have time to go into all that in this book, but you are welcome to go and discover what I believe about all that for yourself, in my "Mirror Word Study Course" called: *"The Gospel In 3-D!"*

But I am getting off track now.

What I was busy saying before I got a little carried away back there with the immenseness of the love of God for us, is that what I want you to see is that before all that, you see, before all these things took place in the work of redemption, while Jesus operated in the flesh, *He operated in His ministry, as a man,*

...He operated, as a man, *in dominion!*

...He operated in the exact *sin dominion* and *sickness dominion*, and *Devil dominion*, that you and I have now been freed to operate in.

As a man, *He operated in that dominion that you and I are now free to operate in.*

...*Because, you see, we have a legal right to operate in it.*

We have a legal right, *to operate in the same dominion that Jesus operated in,* in His earthly ministry ...*because of that gift of righteousness restored.*

You see we are now legally and vitally restored, to that original righteousness; to that innocence we fell from, in that Garden.

I say again: *We are now fully restored, to that glory we lost, there in the Fall.*

Jesus said,

"The same works that I've done, you will do also, and greater!"

"...and greater, yes, exactly the same, and greater, because I only have one pair of hands, but now, I can multiply Myself in My Church, in My saints, in My believers!"

"…yes, greater, because now I go <u>as you</u>, to be made totally one with My Father again; He is <u>your Father</u> also, and I am going there, and I have gone there, to release that authority back unto you,"

"…that's why I said you will now also be able, all of you, to do My works, and greater!" - John 14:12.

Let me just point this out to you perhaps a little more clearly that, **in Jesus' ministry, He demonstrated to the Devil and to Man, the authority and the dominion of the second Adam, the authentic original Adam; the last Adam, also knows as the New Creation Man, or** *the New Man created in His death and brought forth in His resurrection!*

In Jesus' ministry, He came to demonstrate to both the Devil and to Man, the authority and dominion *of an Adam that would not bow the knee!*

Jesus was the last Adam, amen; *the last of the fallen Adamic race.*

He then also became the first born from the dead. He is both the Alpha and Omega, amen. He is the ultimate Preeminent One and *all things conclude in Him!*

But He is not merely an example for us, *but of us!* **In Him, a new race, a new species** *was born, in His resurrection,*

100

In His resurrection, *the one new Man, the new creation Man, was born!*

We, the human race, were re-booted to newness of life in His resurrection!

We were re-booted to a living hope by the resurrection of Jesus Christ from the dead!
- 1 Peter 1:3; Romans 4:25; Romans 6:4; 1 Corinthians 15:17.

Hey, the Devil tried to stop Him from accomplishing what He was sent to accomplish! The Devil kept trying to stop Him, *but he failed!*

Hey, I think the Devil already knew his days were numbered, *when he failed to successfully tempt Jesus, there in the desert!*

You see the Devil knew that, really, *his only chance* was there in the wilderness, *while Jesus was weak and vulnerable.*

If Jesus did, what Adam did there in the Garden, **God's plan would have died there, with Him.**

But no, *He defeated and bound the strong man,* there in the desert; and ultimately there on the cross.

But He first bound the strong man, *by refusing to yield to Sin and its fruit of sin.*

…what I mean by *"He first bound the strong man"* is that He did it in his own person, as a man, He did it as a man; as an example of us, *not for us.* Jesus defeated and bound the strong man, *by not accepting any of his offers …by not accepting Sin …by not entering into sin …by not accepting any inferior identity …by not accepting any other alternative …by not accepting any other way, other than the Father's will, than the Father's wishes, than the Father's original design; than the Father's original truth; than the Father's way.*

Thus, Jesus refused to embrace an inferior identity, and that means that Jesus' life and ministry as a man was out of bounds to the Devil!

You see, Jesus said that **if you bind the strong man,** *then you can go into his house, and plunder his goods.*

And that is exactly what Jesus did on the cross, amen!

He bound the Devil, *because He totally defeated him and stripped him of all his authority,* there on the cross!

He bound the Devil,

…So we may plunder his goods!

But, in a sense, that scripture can also be read as Jesus saying, *"If you first bind the strong man, in your own life, amen, by fully embracing the Father's truth concerning you, and not yielding to Satan's lies and deception and temptation any more, then you can go into that defeated foe's house, and plunder his goods."*

Let's understand it this way, I mean let me just explain it this way,

Let's say, should Jesus have given in to Satan, *and fallen into temptation* ...*should Jesus have sinned* ...and He could have sinned there, amen ...Do you know that? Do you know that Jesus could have sinned there if He wanted to, *but He didn't want to, amen.* Thank God He didn't want to! Thank God he said no to the Devil! ...But He could have sinned; *He was fully capable of yielding to sin, just like us.*

We must not think that, just because Jesus was Jesus, *that He couldn't have sinned.*

Let's face it; *He was human, in every way!*

He became, *a man,* amen!

So, should Jesus have sinned, Satan would have won; *it would have been all over, God's entire plan would have been shipwrecked, and we would still be living under the full dominion of our ignorance and of darkness!*

You know, for years and years they believed that it was impossible for a man to swim across the English Channel, *and then the first guy did it,* **proving them all wrong!**

But now let's say that, afterward, **they discover that this man cheated,** and that, just under the surface of the water, he had like a cable, running all the way, right from the one side to the other side, and here he was, **acting like he was swimming, but in the mean time, it was all a lie;** he was just pulling himself along by this cable, or he was being pulled along by some other motorized power source attached to the cable or something and pulling the cable along, from one side to the other side. **His achievement would immediately lose all authority, you know what I mean, it would not count; it would be canceled out! It would have totally canceled his victory, amen, because he cheated!**

Listen, we must understand the humanity of Jesus Christ!

So often we think,

'Oh well, that was just Jesus, you know, that was just Jesus'

…But listen while we think like that, while we reason like that …**then we'll also think,**

'Well, all those miracles that happened, it happened because He was Jesus, you know, *and we can never possibly walk in any authority like that, you know ...we can't do the same ...and we really can't walk free from sin either.'*

...And we'll think,

*'He lived above sin, **because He was Jesus, you know,** and He was just a unique individual, one of a kind, the one and only Son of God, I mean, He was not just a man, after all He was the Son of God and all that, **and we will never be like Him, I mean, maybe one day in Heaven, but not while we're here on this earth, it's impossible, we are just sinners saved by grace, but sinners none the less!'***

...And the religious Church establishment has been thinking like this, for centuries already, **totally totally defeated, in their own walk, and in their own experience as a Christian,** *because they have bought into this lie, and they have believed it!*

*...**And therefore they have refused to believe what God came to fully reveal and restore to us in the incarnation; in the man, Jesus Christ!***

*...**They have refused to fully believe it and understand it!***

But in the meantime they totally ignore the scriptures like 1 John 4:17, which clearly says that, ***"As He is, so are we, in this world!"***

...And they have refused to fully believe it!

Do you know why they have believed the lie, and bought into it, and held on to it as doctrine?

...Because they want to apologize for their unbelief, and for their pet sins; *they want to have a convenient excuse to keep living an inferior life!*

It is astounding to me, how Christians, *supposedly saved people who love Jesus, who is supposed to believe in Jesus and His successful reconciliation work, and full redemption accomplishment, and be full of faith and power* ...it is astonishing to me, how those Christians, *will fight for their unbelief* ...*they will fight for their right to remain a sinner* ...*because they don't want to get rid of their unbelief,*

'I mean, that's just too much of a challenge brother Rudi; it is easier to remain double-minded and unstable in all my ways, I mean Jesus will understand, after all, I'm only human.'

They will keep on fighting for the right to remain a sinner, *to remain less than,*

...All because they have some pet sins in their life that they do not want to get rid of *and want to keep making excuses for!*

It seems that they still do not understand what Jesus meant when He said, *"**Very truly I tell you, everyone who sins is by their sins made a slave to sin.**"* - John 8:34.

They still do not seem to understand that **what you feed will grow,** and that some things *just aren't worth feeding,* because eventually, your secret nasty little pet habit, that habit that may have started out as a mere little controllable pet devil, **will mature,** *and once it matures **it becomes a real demon that devours you!*** The Devil specializes in using sin to **steal, kill and destroy!**

But hey listen; Jesus is the solution!

He came, and He *fully* identified with Man!

Jesus *fully* identified with the human being; *with you, and with me!*

He *fully* identified with Man!

He walked where you and I walk.

He walked in the flesh, *fully partaking of flesh and blood.*

He walked where you and I walk,

*...**yet free from sin, living above it ...in a place of authority and dominion over the Devil and all his forces of darkness.***

The Bible says that He was tempted, *just like you and I are tempted,*

...*He was tempted, in every way, in every point, just as we are,*

...yet, without sin.

He refused to embrace unbelief! He refused to adopt an inferior fallen identity! He refused to see Himself in any other way than seeing Himself through the eyes of his Father!

He was tempted at times, to do so, amen.

But he refused to see Himself as a mere man!

Listen, I can't tempt you with something, *if you are not interested in it!*

You see because it will not appeal to your person *if it will not appeal to your senses, or if it will not appeal to your will.*

You cannot be tempted, *unless there is a strong appeal in that temptation!*

Jesus didn't yield to the flesh, to the a sin-nature, to the fallen nature; to an inferior identity! *He didn't yield to the Fall at all,* and yet He was a man just like us.

Now that should tell you something about the Fall and about yourself!

108

Jesus came to reveal that the Fall is ultimately a lie; *and that we remained the children of God, made in His image and likeness, <u>in spite of the Fall</u>.*

He came to endorse that God's original design of the human being is intact!

He came to endorse that it remained intact in spite of the Fall.

He didn't have a sin-nature, *and He came to prove that we don't have one either!*

He came to prove that *our identity* **as children of God** *is intact!*

He came to prove that our sin is ultimately the fruit of deception; *the fruit of a lie!*

...We have believed and lived that lie for so long that we have believed it to be the truth about us; *the ultimate truth!*

But just because you believe a lie to be the ultimate truth *doesn't make it so!*

God knows the ultimate truth about us, and He had that truth preserved in the heavenlies; within Himself, and in the fullness of time He revealed that truth to us, in a man; the man Jesus Christ!

If these things are not true, *and were not true to begin with,* then what about people like Abel, and Enoch, **who listened to the truth**

preserved in their own hearts, and to whatever truth they could gain by their forefather, Adam, *and so by faith, by insight and revelation, tapped into their righteousness,* <u>even after the Fall</u>

...And what about people like Abraham, and David **that became friends of God, and walked in some kind of intimate relationship with God, however limited at the time,** but only because of limited light, because the full light, the true light of the world, who enlightens every person, all mankind, have not come into the world and come on the scene yet, *but never the less,* **they were able to tap into something glorious, some future glories,** *which wasn't readily available in their time,* **and yet, they were able to make it theirs, in relationship with God**

...And what about all those who make up the entire Old Testament cloud of witnesses written about in Hebrews 11; men and women of faith, **who by revelation from God saw something, and partook of something, before its time,** *something of old that were to be revealed as new again, in the Messiah; in the person of Jesus Christ!*

The prophets and people of old, they all wrote and spoke *concerning God's coming deliverance; His work of salvation.*

They spoke, and wrote about it, and in part, partook of it for themselves, *that grace that* *was to come to us,* searching intently, and with great care, trying to find out the exact time and circumstances and person, *concerning which the very Spirit of God within them was pointing to,* when He predicted the sufferings of Christ and <u>the subsequent glories that would follow</u>.

It was indeed revealed to them that they were not merely serving themselves, but indeed us, when they spoke about and wrote about, *the very things that are now being declared to us, by those who have seen and understood and grasped the truth of the Gospel, by the help of the Holy Spirit of truth sent from heaven; from out of the unseen spirit realm of reality.*

Even angels long to look into these things and grasp them, *but it is not for them, it is for us to hear and comprehend and live!*

Therefore, Peter says, *"With minds that are alert and fully sober, set your hope fully upon the grace of God that is being brought to you, at this current time, within the revelation of Jesus Christ, who was sent to us from heaven to reveal these very things to us."* - 1 Peter 1:10-13

So, these things are true, and Jesus came to reveal them and redeem them.

Jesus came, *and he didn't have a sin-nature ...but He had a mind, and he also had a body <u>just like ours</u> ...and He was* *strongly appealed to, by the Devil, <u>just like</u>* *<u>we are</u>!* *...He was strongly appealed to!* **The Devil made a strong appeal!**

Jesus was strongly tempted! He was tempted *in every point ...<u>just as we are</u>!*

But praise God, He said,

"...the evil one <u>has nothing</u> in me!"

...And he wasn't <u>lying</u> amen!

No, He could say these things *with all authority* **...all because Jesus, <u>who fully</u>** **<u>represents us in every way</u>,** *(even more so than Adam, amen)* **...this Jesus of ours,** *did not have a sin-nature.*

...That's why I do not believe in such a thing as Man, *having a sin-nature.*

Man was not designed or made *with a sinful-nature,* **amen!**

Hey, Jesus conquered the Devil *in His humanity as a man!*

He did not partake of some secret something we don't have!

He didn't have some kind of secret weapon!

You see, understanding this truth, *puts you in dominion!*

He only partook of, and stood *in that authority, that he had, as a man, because of his righteousness* ...because of our original righteousness still intact!

You see, faith, is in dominion!

Righteousness is in dominion!

The truth of your righteousness; *the truth of your design and your identity, is in dominion!*

You see, the truth of these things fully restored to us; *the truth of our righteousness fully restored to us,* is in dominion!

It places us in dominion!

Our faith about these things, *places us in dominion!*

Our faith is in dominion!

Faith; the faith of God revealed in Jesus is in total dominion!

"Resist the devil, steadfast in the Faith; refuse his lies, remain steadfast in the Faith, and he will flee from you!" - James 4:7; 1 Peter 5:9.

He will have no choice in the matter!

"This is the victory that overcomes the world, even our faith!" - 1 John 5:4.

...But you see, and I emphasize again; it's not our faith, it's not of us, it's the faith of God that causes us to live in victory!

...And the faith of God has been imparted to us, through the truth of the gospel ...it has become our faith!

Through understanding and grasping exactly who we truly are ...and getting the full revelation of what exactly Jesus revealed and restored to us, in that work of redemption ...the faith of God, has become our faith!

You see, faith, is in dominion! The faith of God, is in total absolute dominion!

Faith always defeats flesh!

Listen that Law of identification, works through <u>faith</u>.

Identification *by faith,* is an extremely powerful law ...*and it will rule whoever submits to it.*

...So you might as well use it to your advantage.

...But you must submit to it correctly.

Identifying yourself with fallen Adam, *keeps you bound,*

...but, identifying yourself with Christ Jesus, *sets you free, and keeps you free!*

....*So, rather identify yourself with Christ Jesus, than with fallen Adam, amen!*

This was Paul's conclusion in Galatians 5:16-20, he says, (and I am quoting out of the Mirror Study Bible this time):

5:16 I conclude: Engage your spirit; engage your inner thoughts with the truth of your true spirit identity as children of God, and allow that understanding, that very faith of God to be the dominant influence in your daily walk and see for yourself how it defeats the cravings of flesh.

The footnote there in the Mirror Study Bible reads:

(Spirit is satisfied by the agape love-law; the revelation of grace – flesh on the other hand craves to prove and gratify itself by the DIY law. **Faith always defeats flesh.**)

5:17 While the law of works still features in your mind, it is a catalyst to disaster; you are caught in the middle of a war zone, wanting to do the things that you desire by design, but finding the flesh in strong resistance to what the spirit desires.

115

Then the footnote again:

(The two trees in the Garden represent the flesh and the spirit, thus it also represents two opposing systems or forces of influence ..Also two separate mindsets. While the tree of life represents the inner-life of our design, the "I-am-not-tree" or what can be referred to as the DIY-tree is extremal to the real person; **but whilst hosted, *like a virus, its influence becomes unavoidable and very visible.*** Paul compares the fruit of righteousness by faith, working through love, versus the works of the flesh and guilt which is nothing other than one's own performance based on obligation, guilt and willpower. - See Romans 3:27, also Romans 7. And while you're at it, remember this: **the war is over! It's already won!** Now, instead of thinking that you're in a war, engage your thoughts with throne room realities instead! - Colossians 3:1-3. Always remember; your victory rests in the triumph of Jesus! - See Ephesians 6 and 2 Corinthians 10:3-6; also 2 Corinthians 12:7-10 for that matter.) And please read it in the Mirror Study Bible; it is most clear there.

5:18 To be acquainted with the prompting of your spirit [faith] is to be free from the law [of personal performance].

Footnote:

(The word, AGESTHE, comes from, AGOO, and it is written in the Present Passive tense –

116

thus translated as: **continual prompting**.
See Galatians 3:3.)

5:19 The typical lifestyle wherever a legalistic judgmental attitude prevails, against oneself and inevitably then others also, is one where sexual sins are rampant! In that negative degrading self-destructing environment anything goes: fornication, adultery, even outrageous licentiousness and all kinds of filthiness.

5:20 Then there is also the inevitable worshipping of a distorted image of oneself that takes place; which is what idolatry is all about; drugs, hatred, constant conflict, jealous suspicions, violent outbursts of rage, everyone for themselves is the result, and it brings about a cut-throat competitive world, where people are trampling on others to get to the top, and where dissension, heresy, and manipulating people's minds with false teachings run rampant.

I love what the footnote adds:

(The flesh is not your "lower nature," *it is the fruit of partaking of another knowledge, other that the knowledge of God.* It is the fruit of partaking in a lie, and the inevitable deception of oneself. It is the fruit of the "**I-am-not**" tree system; it is a mindset governed by a sense of lack and desperately trying to do life **by sheer willpower,** *independent of your*

Source.) - Galatians 5:16-20 [Mirror Study Bible].

Paul says a little earlier on there in Galatians 5:1,

"Hey, it was for freedom that Christ has set us free! No longer to be subject to a yoke of slavery of any kind!"

The absolute freedom that is so beautifully on exhibit in the person of Jesus Christ *belongs equally to every single person on this planet!*

No, not the freedom to express our confusion, or the lie; the supposed "fallen nature" inherited from Adam, *for that is no freedom at all!*

It was for real freedom that Christ has come to set us free: The freedom to fully express the beauty of our original most amazing authentic design; the very spectacular image and likeness of the glorious invisible God, our origin; our true Father!

The beauty of that glory again made visible in us; our very identity as children of God revealed and put on open display in us – that most authentic Christ-life enjoyed and exhibited in us, *that is the true freedom Christ has come to set us free to enjoy, experience, and exhibit <u>to the max</u>!*

Chapter 5

We Do Not Have A Sin-nature!

Listen, Man's true nature is not the "sin-nature" or "lower nature." Man does not have a "sin-nature" and Man most certainly does not have two natures either!

The "sin-nature" or "lower nature" is all the fruit of the lie we have embraced and believed and lived!

It is all the fruit of the "I-am-not" tree; that system of thought, that stronghold, that mindset, that false identity *we inherited in the fall.*

The so called "sin-nature" *is an outside force* that came from the Devil; and from self-deception.

…It's his nature, *not our nature* …*not our true nature.*

That false identity, that nature, that force, that virus came in through the Law of Identification, *but it can also be undone,* through the Law of Identification!

The word "SIN" is an old Anglo-Saxon word. It was a term used in the sport of archery. In that sport, if one were to aim at the bullseye on a target, and yet the arrow would miss its target when released, that shot would be called a "sin" shot.

Thus, to "SIN" means, **to miss the mark.**

The Greek word for "SIN" is the word, HAMARTIA and it comes from the presupposition HA, and the word, MEROS. HA always indicates a negative, such as **no,** or **not to,** and MEROS speaks of **that which has inherent value or merit.** Thus the word HAMARTIA refers to **something worthless, or a non entity; involving oneself with that which is absolutely worthless or has no merit; it is of very little to no value!**

That is why, when referring to SIN, a "lie" or "un-truth" also immediately comes to mind, *because, unlike truth, a lie has no inherent value or substance!*

To SIN is therefore, **to live outside of ones original design!**

Thus, SIN means, **to believe and embrace a lie about oneself!**

It is to see yourself in a way other than the way God sees you!

It is to think less of yourself than what God thinks of you!

Thus, it is to adopt *an inferior identity!*

You see, SIN and its "nature" may have set up camp inside of Man, because of the Fall *...but it was still an alien force ...foreign to our real nature; our true nature, our true design.*

That "sin-nature" through the Fall *set up government over Man;*

...It became a law that dominated us.

Paul refers to it as, *the Law of Sin and Death.*

...It was a law, *a force* that exerted its negative influence upon Man's nature, *against the true design of that nature!*

That is what the "sin-nature" or the "sinful-nature" is; *it is the law of Sin and death in operation; it is the nature of SIN at work; <u>it's the original lie at work</u>.*

...It is the Devil's own twisted nature.

It is evil, and that evil, that nature exerts itself ...it tries to influence, our thinking, and our beliefs, *and therefore our nature, against our true design, our true nature; the true design of our nature!*

It is interesting to note that the word for "evil" in the Greek, as in *"the tree of the knowledge of good and evil"* is the word, PANEROS and it refers to **all manner of hardships, labors, toil and frustration.**

That is exactly what the twisted nature of the Devil and of SIN and of Religion is all about!

I say again: The Devil's very name is the word DIABOLOS in the Greek. DIA means **through,** and BOLOS means **to cast down, to trip,** or **to fall.** That the very name of the Devil refers to **that influence that comes to us *through the fall* to manipulate and dominate and try and rule us.**.

It is also interesting to note that Satan's name is directly tied to *"the knowledge of good and evil"* His name is directly tied to that tree; to that **other knowledge, *that accusation and lie introduced to us in the garden which brought about the Fall.***

Satan, or SATANOS in the Greek literally means **accusation or accuser.**

Jesus referred to him as the father of lies.

Satan came to introduce the lie that says, *"I-am-not ...therefore, I-have-to-become"*

It all sounds good; *it doesn't sound so bad does it?* But it's an introduction to poison.

...It's an introduction to "evil;" to a worthless mentality of inferiority, projecting itself as superior, in an effort to try and gain superiority.

...Thus, it is the introduction to an inferior life, filled with all kinds of hardships, and

worthless labors, and toil that can only lead to frustration *and an absolute inevitable inferiority complex.*

So, in Romans Paul explains how the "sin-nature" came into the world *as a foreign entity.* - Romans 5:12.

...**And it set up a stronghold inside of Man ...thus, ruling over Man,** *negatively influencing us all the time, polluting and corrupting our nature, against the true design of that nature; making us slaves of sin!*

You can read all about it in Romans 7.

But, you can also go and read *what happened to that supposed "sin-nature;" to Sin and its nature, through the death of Jesus, and how we are freed from it by what is revealed and accomplished in Him!*

You will find that in Romans 5, 6 and 8.

You see, once you realize that Jesus did not die FOR Man, *but AS Man,* **only then can you finally begin to comprehend the gospel and partake in its power!**

Whatever we thought we were, *could never match what God always knew we are!* - Jeremiah 1:5; 1 Corinthians 13:12.

What God always knew we are *is exactly what God revealed and restored in Jesus!*

Hey, you can only live **one** of two lives: **a frustrated one** ...*or a fulfilled one!*

It is *our reference of ourselves* that makes all the difference in the world. Make the success of the cross *your only reference!*

There is such a big difference between law and grace! Law amounts to mere window-shopping, *while grace is mirror-gazing at its best!*

Ha... ha... ha...

Hallelujah!

Hey, we need to clearly understand at this point that when we read these Scriptures, this letter from Paul, to the Romans, he does not *speak of, (or condone the idea of), two natures in one man!*

That is nothing other than confusing religious nonsense; law-language at its worst. *It is most certainly not an idea either Paul or God promotes!*

Throughout human history religion often got confused *when they looked at someone's conduct or behavior,* especially if that person is supposed to be a so called *"born again"* believer.

...And so they thought, 'Well, something doesn't line up here, so, maybe it's just the old nature that is still manifesting'

124

Listen, if that was true, then that would mean that half of that person would go to Heaven, *while the other half goes to Hell!*

Ha... ha... ha...

Listen, Romans 7:25 can be quite confusing in some of our English translations, ***because of the way it is was miss-translated*** *out of the original text, based on the translator's particular bent, or preference, or miss-understanding, or thought-process and mindset at the time.*

It says,

*"...**so then, in myself, in my mind, I am a slave to God's Law, but in the sinful-nature I am a slave to the law of Sin**"*

You see, many of our translations, ***because of inaccurate theology, and therefore wrong understanding in the minds of the translators,*** many of them, use the words, *"**sinful-nature**"* or, *"**sin-nature**,"* here in Romans 7, **but it is nowhere to be found *in the original text; in the original Greek ...it is not in the Greek at all!***

Hey listen, there is no *"sinful-nature!"*

You can't have two natures!

Jesus says that *not even trees have two natures,* amen!

In Luke 6:44 Jesus says:

"For men do not gather figs from thorns, nor do they gather grapes from a bramble bush!"

And in James 3:11 & 12 we read,

"Does a spring send forth fresh and bitter water from the same opening?"

"Or can a fig tree, my brethren, bear olives, or a grapevine bear figs?"

No!

Amen! Hallelujah!

Listen man, if you have two natures inside of you, *then half of you will just have to go to Hell, while only half of you, and hopefully the good half, will make it into Heaven.*

Ha… ha… ha…

…**Or,** *you'll have to go to Heaven and Hell at the same time!* …**And that is going to be terribly difficult for you to handle!**

Ha… ha… ha…

Oh, hallelujah!

Or is it:: Ouch!

Ha…ha…ha…

So, go ahead and change your translations wherever it uses that phrase, *"sin-nature"* or, *"sinful-nature,"* You have God's permission on that, **because it is not in the Greek!**

Those who still talk that way *don't know what they're talking about, and they have no clue about spirit-truth.*

*…**Nor do they really understand new creation realities!***

Listen, what part of,

*"…**therefore, since you are in Christ, you are a new creation, the old things have passed away, behold, all things have become new,"***

…what part of **that** do they not understand?

The very nature that identified Man as a sinner, and a fallen creature, *is challenged,* in the gospel.

Listen, who got lost?

Man did, *not God!*

Where did Man get off track?

In his thinking! It started in his thinking!

*…**And because Man got off track, in his thinking, his quality of life began to reveal it!***

Listen, as a man thinks in his heart, *so is he!* - Proverbs 23:7.

So often we sit and we put up with the frustration of *an unfulfilled life,*

…And so we end up just accepting the fact that the thief came to steal, kill, and destroy, and the Fall happened, and here we are now, still,

…but at least we can blame the old Devil for our state of being!

And we can write volumes of books about the Devil and his power *…as if his ability is so enormous that he is in the end, the one that should actually be celebrated, and praised, and worshipped, instead of Jesus!*

But then we end up missing the whole good news message!

John 10:10 doesn't stop with, *"…**the thief came to steal, kill, and destroy**"*

No, it doesn't stop there!

Jesus interrupts that statement and says,

*"…**BUT**, I came, that you might have life, and have it more abundantly."*

He came to give that life more abundantly *to the same person* that *saw, so powerfully,* how the enemy comes to steal, kill, and destroy.

128

Jesus came to give life more abundantly *to the same person* that *became, so persuaded,* about that enemy's power to steal, kill and destroy!

Listen, if Man comes out of God, then he remains God's property; *God's family.*

He remains God's, amen! - Ephesians 3:14.

A friend of mine preaches a lot in the prisons, and I laughed when he shared how he asks the prisoners,

'If someone stole something, at what point does it become that person's property? I mean, how long must he have it in his possession, before it becomes his, if ever?'

They always all laugh and say, *"It never becomes theirs!"*

Yet, we Christians, have handed over ownership of mankind, *to the father of lies* …While all the while Psalm 24:1 clearly says that,

"The earth is the Lord's, and the fullness thereof, the world, and those who dwell in it!"

Man is God's possession; *His inheritance!*

John 1 says that,

"He came to His own!"

God came to His own!

We are His very own!

God is not in a negotiation struggle with Satan, over the human race, *or the human being!*

God's claim, God's right over Man, *remains valid forever; for all eternity!*

Only two chapters after Jesus said to the Pharisees that they are of their father the devil, (because they embraced his lies), he quotes Psalm 82:6 *to the same audience*, there in John 10:34, and it says,

"I say, ye are gods, all of you are sons of the Most High!"

The problem was that they have forgotten the Rock that they were all hewn from; *the God who gave them birth.* - Deuteronomy 32:3-6; Isaiah 51:1; Matthew 16:15-19; 1 Peter 2:4-6.

What was God's purpose, His mission, His commission in Christ?

To reconcile the human race to Himself!

To reconcile *the human being* to Himself!

Behold the Lamb of God that takes away the sin *of the world* ...not put it on ice temporarily.

…He takes it away!

…And so, if we have a message, then this must be our message!

If we want to say something to Man, anything, *that will bring Man to the conviction of faith,* to the same persuasion, to the same conclusion of the gospel, then we must tell Man, *not how guilty he still is, but we must tell him,* <u>*how innocent he now is*</u> *…how <u>free</u> he now is,* because of what was revealed and accomplished in the incarnation and successful work of redemption!

The Fall can no longer be our reference!

You see the Law already showed to Man, how terribly, totally, sinful, he has become, through the Fall.

The Law already convinced and convicted Man of, how guilty, and deserving of punishment he is, *how much of a sinner he is, how empty he is, how unfulfilled he is.*

The Law correctly defined the Fall, *but couldn't fix the Fall.*

But here comes the good news!

God, in the fullness of time, in Jesus Christ, and now in the gospel, comes *to persuade,* <u>the same Man, the same person</u>, *of how complete his salvation and deliverance is; how finalized his court case is!*

God acted to the favor and absolute benefit *of every person,* in the obedience of Jesus Christ!

'Where does that old sinful-nature in Man come from then, brother Rudi?'

Listen I say again, **the trouble did not start in the nature, *but, in the mind!***

Man got lost, in his thinking, first, and he began to partake of, *another knowledge, other than, the knowledge and truth of God.*

He got lost, in his way of looking at things, and reasoning about things!

Man lost his way, in his thinking, *and his nature began to express it!*

A man's nature is what his thoughts are; *what his thinking, what his mentality is!*

Man lost his way, in the spirit of his mind and in his reference of himself!

But, the Fall can never again be our reference!

Jesus is our only accurate reference; *our only reference!*

Listen, I say again, **the Devil is not the father of Man;** *of the human being ...He did not design even one cell in one body!*

He is only the father of deception; *the father of lies, you see!*

...But while I take the lie, and entertain the lie, *the lie takes hold of me ...just like alcohol and like drugs ...or like a virus!*

...So, the lie I embrace manifests itself in me. Its character is like a virus!

The virus doesn't take on the person, and become the person. I mean, *the person doesn't become the virus.*

No, the person is the person, and the virus is the virus!

The person remains the person, *but the virus manifests itself in the person, no matter who the person is!*

...And when that snot-sickness lays a hold of you, ha... ha... ha... *it isn't pretty my friend ... it's plain miserable!*

Listen that thing, that bug, that Sin, *is looking for a host!*

No real doctor, worth his wage, will walk into a room full of sick people *and start slapping the guy who is coughing, and telling him to stop coughing immediately,*

'Listen, this is your last cough, or else!'

Ha… ha… ha…

No!

He knows how to distinguish the person from the symptoms,

…And he knows how to treat that sickness, and get rid of the symptoms!

…He doesn't blame the person, amen!

It doesn't even matter how sick the person is, or for how long he has been sick, *never at any point does the symptom become the person!*

You can never become the flu!

You can get the flu, and be afflicted by the flu, *but the flu is the flu, and you are you!*

This beautiful body God gave us, and this image of God in us …this soul and spirit, *can get so easily polluted,* with stupid idiotic things, *thoughts and beliefs and passions* …and so we think,

*'Wow man, oh well, I guess we are all but human after all. Thank God, in Heaven He will finally sort it all out, **but in the mean time, I will just have to live in perpetual frustration, embarrassment, and the occasional outright shame!***'

...As if the cross didn't succeed, as if Jesus didn't succeed in God's mission, *to take away and remove sin from us forever!*

I suggest to you, that Jesus came, *in the flesh,* and lived, *as a man, free from sin, free from that original lie and its influence*

...And then, in His cross, *He freed us, to do the same!*

If we dare to *discover* the cross, the message of the cross, *the simplicity* of the cross, *the simplicity* of the gospel, *the simplicity* of the power of the gospel, we will be able to say with Paul,

"I am not embarrassed; I am not ashamed of this gospel!"

I am not a sinner anymore!

I don't have a sin-nature!

I am a new creation in Christ, *as revealed in Him and His work of redemption!*

I am a child of God!

I am a partaker of the Divine nature!

I am able to give, full expression, to the image and likeness of God in me; *to the very nature of God in me!*

I do not have to yield to sin, anymore … *because I am under the influence, and the power, of grace; I am under the influence and power of what God accomplished, in the grace of that one man, Jesus Christ!*

"By the grace of God, I am what I am!"

*'Sin shall not be my master, **because I am under grace!**"*

*"…**His grace towards me was not in vain!**"*

Hallelujah!

Thank you Jesus!

Chapter 6

Righteousness And Anointing!

Let's delve right back into our subject of the humanity of Jesus, there are some more things I want to emphasize about His humanity and how it now relates to us.

I said earlier that *we must understand the humanity of Jesus!*

He was tempted, like us, in every point!

And yet, He conquered the Devil, *in His humanity, as a man.*

He did not have some hidden secret!

He didn't partake of some kind of secret weapon!

His only weapon was that *He fully agreed with His Father over who He was.*

He agreed with the Father *over His identity as child of God!*

He *fully agreed with His Father over His true nature.*

He believed He was a partaker of the Divine nature!

He only partook of, and stood on the authority, that he had, *because of that* *righteousness* **…because of** *His* **righteousness;** *because of what He believed about His real identity!*

You see, that truth, about His real identity, about His true nature, is in dominion!

Righteousness is in dominion!

That was absolutely the only authority He had.

You see religion teaches that,

Jesus is the perfect example, *and we've got to now try and live up to that example, and try and imitate Him, to the best of our ability you see,*

…and they also teach that,

God works on merits you know, and if you have finally become, say like 50% or so, *like Jesus* **…then maybe, God will just have pity on you** …and just say to you,

"Wow man, you've tried so hard, and you've really impressed Me, you see, so now I can reward you with power and what not, and you just go for it, from now on, okay, all

kinds of miracles will now follow your ministry!"

...and then, suddenly, (...this is what they teach now,)

Suddenly, one day in Heaven, *then suddenly also, you will be like Jesus, just automatically, just like that,* when you die and you now go to Heaven ...*if you make it to heaven that is!*

...That is how they have interpreted and thought this thing out, you see!

Listen, Jesus was not just a great example, to try and strive after, and to try and imitate, and try and be like!

He was not an example for you, *but of you!*

He was not just a great example; *He came to impart that life into our hearts* ...**And listen, with that impartation of truth, and life, *He puts that ability within us, both to will, and to do, amen!***

Jesus said,

"My words are spirit, and life!"

With the truth that comes to us, *an ability to live that truth, gets awakened in us, at the same time,*

...**it is awakened, *by the Spirit of Truth,***

...by the <u>Holy</u> Spirit,

That power of the Holy Spirit, gets imparted, *to awaken my faith,*

...and to awaken that energy in me, to <u>live</u> that truth!

God backs up His word, *with power,* **amen!**

Faith becomes the link.

...And that faith gets imparted, and comes alive in me, by the Spirit impartation of truth!

Listen, truth, and the anointing, are absolutely connected.

Righteousness, and the anointing, are absolutely connected!

Thus, Jesus walked in righteousness, and the anointing!

You see Jesus walked in a righteous relationship with God!

What is righteousness?

To be righteous means, **to measure yourself correctly, accurately, according to God's original design; God's opinion of you** *... according to that true spirit-identity, which God has given you* **...not your natural identity, or that fallen-identity, amen!**

Thus, the Hebrew word for righteousness, *'TZEDEK'* comes from the word, *'TZADOK,'* and it speaks of, **the wooden beam, or cross beam in a scale of balances.**

You see, when an object on one side of the scale is **measured against something** on the other side of the scale **and a match is found,** *the wooden cross beam reaches equilibrium and is then referred to as righteous; it has effectively reached a point of righteousness, or being righteous.* It therefore **declares** that **the measure by which an item was measured by** *is an accurate measure.*

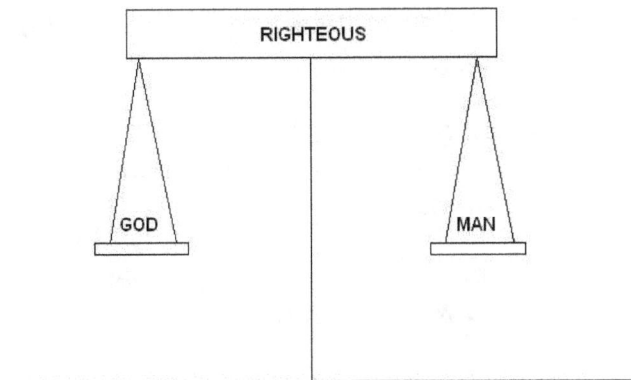

Actually that word, *"righteousness"* comes from an old Anglo-Saxon word, *"right-wise-ness,"* meaning, **to be wise concerning that** *which is right, or true, or accurate!*

In other words, **to be wise concerning the knowledge of your true spirit identity!**

...To be wise concerning your true design!

...To be wise concerning the love of God for you, *to understand that He is your Daddy ...and that you were made, (brought forth from within Him) to be like Him and to enjoy an intimate friendship and love relationship with Him, as Father!*

...a relationship of no condemnation, no guilt, no inferiority,

...it is based upon, His embrace and acceptance and welcome of you, in His presence!

...it speaks of equality and mutual adoration in relationship!

No condemnation, no guilt, no inferiority, and <u>actual</u> innocence, are then also, *the <u>fruit</u> of righteousness!*

You see, Jesus walked in a righteous relationship with His Father.

...That means, He walked in a true relationship, *not a fake dysfunctional relationship!*

...He walked in a righteous relationship; *a relationship of no condemnation, no guilt, no inferiority,*

...a relationship of true innocence!

...and He enjoyed that innocence in his conscience and in His walk.

...and you see, because of that, *He could receive and flow in the anointing!*

See, the moment death comes in, in your relationship with God, *you lose that anointing,*

...you loose your ability to flow in the anointing!

In 1 John 2:20 & 21, and 24-27, John talks about *understanding that which was from the beginning,*

...and that we have been anointed, to understand these things.

In fact he says that *we have all received that anointing, from the Holy One, from the Holy Spirit.*

He says, *"If that truth, which was from the beginning, abides in you,"*

"...then, you will abide in the Son, and in the Father,"

...and thus, you will also, therefore, abide in the Holy Spirit, and in the anointing.

He goes on to say that,

"…the anointing, which you received from Him, abides in you, and you don't need instructions on how it functions (My sheep hear My voice, amen)*, so you don't need anyone to teach you, because His anointing teaches you, about everything,"*

"… and that anointing is, the truth," he says,

"…and it is true,"

"...and it is no lie,"

"…so, just as it (as the truth) *has taught you, abide in Him!"* he says.

In this scripture John basically lets us know that **truth is the anointing!**

It's our connection to the Spirit of God.

And listen, just as truth and the Spirit of God is inseparably linked, truth, and righteousness also, *are absolutely connected!* **Thus, truth and righteousness** *are inseparably linked!*

...**Therefore, truth, and the anointing,** *are also absolutely connected and inseparably linked* ...*because righteousness and the anointing are absolutely connected, and inseparably linked!*

Now listen to me acutely carefully now,

...The moment you drift away, *from the truth of your righteousness restored to you in Jesus,*

...and start embracing a lie again, an alternative, an alternate identity, *you lose the anointing,*

...and you lose your ability to flow in the anointing!

It takes sensitivity, to the voice of truth within you,

...to the voice of your righteousness,

...and it takes sensitivity, to the voice of God within you, to the voice of His abiding Spirit, *to walk in the anointing; to flow in the anointing!*

Jesus walked, in a sensitive relationship, with God His Father.

Jesus walked, in sensitivity, to the Holy Spirit within Him.

Jesus walked, in a sensitive relationship, with the Spirit of Truth.

The Holy Spirit, and the Spirit of Truth, is synonymous, amen!

It's the same Spirit, amen.

He is the very Spirit of God Himself!

Jesus walked in sensitivity!

He walked sensitive to His spirit.

...to the Spirit of God within His spirit.

He who is joined to the Lord, who is the Spirit, *is one spirit with Him,* amen!

Thus, Jesus walked in sensitivity!

He walked, sensitively, to His righteousness,

...sensitive, to righteousness.

He walked, sensitive, to God His Father!

He walked, sensitive to that knowledge and that relationship.

Thus, Jesus walked, *in righteousness ...and the anointing!*

He walked, in a righteousness-consciousness; in a righteousness based relationship with God! Thus, He walked in a righteous relationship; a relationship that had everything to do with righteousness.

You see, the moment you are not actually walking, in your righteousness; *in your true identity as a child of God,*

...walking, conscious of your righteousness,

146

...conscious, of that precious truth,

...the truth of innocence and identity restored;

...the truth that you have been made righteous, and are righteous,

...The minute you stop walking *conscious* of your righteousness, *conscious* of that precious truth,

...you lose the anointing,

...you loose your ability to flow in the anointing ...and you can no longer flow in the anointing!

...And, the moment, you are no longer walking, *in actual righteousness,*

...in the <u>fruit</u> of righteousness,

...the <u>fruit</u> of your true spirit identity,

...in the <u>truth</u>, of who you are,

I.e. when you start to embrace a lie,

...and when you start to embrace, an inferior fleshly identity,

...and you start to walk, in that alternative identity ...that false, inferior identity ...that false, inferior life ...yielding to sin,

...When you are no longer walking, in actual righteousness ...*you lose your anointing,*

...*I mean, you can no longer flow in the anointing ...you loose your ability to <u>flow</u> in the anointing!*

You see, you don't actually lose it; *you don't lose God's Spirit,*

...*but you can no longer operate in the anointing!*

...*you can no longer operate, like you should be able to operate, in the anointing!*

...*because you grieve God's Spirit,*

...*you grieve the Spirit within you,*

...*your own spirit,*

...*and now you have, a broken relationship,*

...*or at best, a dysfunctional relationship,*

...*and something within you dies ...and so, something between you and God dies,*

...*because something within you, and between you and God, already died!*

He hasn't left you, because He promised to never leave you nor forsake you,

…but there isn't that sweet fellowship, you used to have,

…and you can no longer really flow in the anointing, like you used to.

…you lose the anointing!

…you lose your ability to interact and flow with the anointing,

…with the Spirit of God!

Do you remember Saul, King Saul?

He was anointed as king,

…but when his heart changed, and he began to violate his conscience and live in sin, and sinned against God,

…he didn't immediately lose his position in the natural; his authority as king,

…as far as people are concerned anyway,

…that came later,

…but he lost his authority, in the spirit,

…he lost, the impact, of his ministry.

…and his kingship began to wane.

Something died on the inside of him, and therefore something died between him and God,

...and death began to set in, in his ministry,

...the sun was setting on his authority, and his kingship!

He lost his authority!

He lost *the impact* of his ministry,

...his ministry was bound to have impact!

...it had an impact!

But now you see, *sin is also bound to have an impact,*

...it's bound to have an impact,

...and it impacted him,

...and it impacted his intimate relationship with God; their intimacy,

...and it impacted his ministry!

He was still anointed king,

...but the anointing could no longer demonstrate in his life!

...it was no longer recognized,

...it no longer carried authority,

...he was no longer recognized, in the spirit realm, as having authority!

...because, he was no longer walking in intimate fellowship with God,

...his relationship with God had become dysfunctional.

In John 15:4-6 Jesus said,

"Abide in Me, and I in you."

"As the branch cannot bear fruit by itself, unless it abides in the vine, neither can you, unless you abide in Me."

"I am the vine, you are the branches. He who abides in Me, and I in him, he it is that bears much fruit, for apart from Me you can do nothing!"

"If a man does not abide in Me, he is no longer attached and therefore withers"

You see, it is extremely important for us, to fully understand, *the anointing.*

The anointing is God's definition of ministry!

...without the anointing, there is no real ministry!

Anointing is God's approval of genuine intimate fellowship with you!

Anointing is God's recognition.

...it's God's recognition of ministry!

...God's acknowledgment of ministry,

...His acknowledgment of you!

...His acknowledgment of you, in that realm of ministry!

...spirit ministry,

...ministry in spirit dimension!

...ministry by the Spirit,

...real ministry,

...Holy Spirit ministry,

...where God anoints your words, and the truth coming out of your mouth!

...where God anoints your public praying over people, and prophesying, and laying hands on the sick,

I am talking about His virtue, His power, His Holy Spirit enablement, that virtue which begins to work through your ministry,

...it begins to flow out of you and issue forth from your life!

You see, God acknowledged Jesus, in the spirit-realm.

He gave recognition to Jesus' ministry.

He gave His personal approval to Jesus' ministry!

...On what grounds?

Jesus *fully embraced* His righteousness!

...the fruit of it, the fruit of that embrace, the fruit of His faith, was a righteous intimate relationship with God!

He walked, in righteous relationship with God; in intimacy with God!

You see, God can't just give recognition and acknowledgment and approval,

He had to have legal grounds, totally legal grounds, actual legal grounds,

...and you see, God gives approval and recognition and acknowledgment of ministry,

...on the basis of righteousness,

...on the legal actual grounds, of someone being righteous, and fully embracing and living in that righteousness; in that identity, and that identification and intimacy with God,

...enjoying their righteousness, enjoying intimacy with God, enjoying being His child; His bride ...and actually living righteous ...as the fruit, of their persuasion

153

and conviction, in that truth of righteousness and innocence!

So you see, on the legal grounds of righteousness, God can release anointing!

...on the legal grounds, of actual righteousness ...actually living righteous, and walking in intimacy with God, as the fruit of faith!

1 John 3:6-10

"No one, who abides in Him, continue in sins. No one, who continue in sins, has either seen Him, or known Him."

"Little children, let no one deceive you, (so let me make this clear, so no one can deceive you!) *He who lives in righteousness; I mean they who truly embrace the truth, believing that they are righteous, fully embracing the knowledge of their righteousness, of the fact that they are children of God, fully reconciled with God, and enjoy their righteousness, and therefore actually <u>live</u> that righteousness, and lives righteous, as Jesus is righteous, manifesting their original design, manifesting the image and likeness of God, manifesting the Divine nature; they are righteous!"*

"He who continues to deliberately sin and commit to Sin, living by a false inferior identity, is of the Devil and is living a lie, just like the Devil does; for the Devil has
154

sinned from the beginning, it's his nature, and now they have made a lie their nature too. And, you see, this is the exact reason the Son of God appeared. The very reason for His appearing was to destroy the influence of the Devil upon us, and the works of the Devil in our lives, and in this world."

"No one born of God continues to relate to Sin, and therefore continue to commit sins; for God's nature abides in him, and he cannot sin; it's no longer his identity; he simply cannot continue in sins; because he is born of God and has embraced his true identity as child of God."

"By this it may be clearly seen who have actually embraced being the children of God, and who are still deceived, being influenced by the Devil, and acting as children of the Devil;"

"...whomever does not embrace righteousness and enjoy his righteousness, and walk in the fruit of that righteousness; and therefore also genuinely loving his brother, is not of God"

I think it is important for us at this point to see and comprehend that Jesus did not just walk, in so called, *"obedience to God;"* some kind of religious obedience to God,

…He did not just walk in obedience to some legalistic religious laws and rules and regulations.

That is not what "obedience to God" is all about!

Yes, Jesus walked in obedience to God, *don't get me wrong!*

But listen now, *He walked in relational obedience!*

He walked in the obedience of faith!

He walked in accurate relationship with the truth of His righteousness!

He walked in complete relationship with God, because of His embrace of the truth!

He walked in sensitivity!

He walked sensitively to God His Father,

…to that Spirit of truth, and the Spirit of faith; that Spirit of God within Him!

He walked in sensitive relationship with His <u>Father</u>!

It is so beautiful there in John 5 where Jesus says,

"I do nothing of My own authority,"

"...of My own initiative even,"

"I do nothing on My own,"

"I do everything in sensitive relationship to the Father,"

"I am so aware of His presence!"

"None of this is Me,"

"...of Myself I can do nothing!"

"It is actually the anointing,"

"...it is His anointing,"

"...His Spirit,"

"...it is actually the Father Himself that does these things, through Me,"

"He does His work, in Me, and through Me!"

"We are so one, that we flow together!"

"I in Him, and Him in Me."

"His Spirit within Me, is the flow within Me."

"My desires, are not My own!"

"We flow together!"

Let's just look at it quickly there.

John Chapter 5 and verse 19,

"Jesus said to them, 'Truly, truly, I say to you, **the Son can do nothing of His own accord,"**

*"...***but only what He sees the Father doing;"**

*"...***for whatever the Father does, that the Son does likewise."**

Verse 20,

"For the Father loves the Son, and shows Him all that He is doing,"

*"...***and greater works than these will He yet show Him, that you may marvel."**

Verse 21,

"For as the Father raises the dead and gives them life, so also the Son desires to give life, and so, gives life to everyone!"

Verse 22,

"The Father judges no one, but has given all judgment (of God's enemies; the forces of darkness) to the Son,"

Verse 23,

*"...***so that all may honor the Son,"**

(...**because of the ministry of truth, the ministry of deliverance from the Devil's lies He brings, and the deliverance from the**

bondage of sickness and disease He brings!)

"...just as they honor the Father! (or should honor the Father who sent Him)"

"...so that all may honor the Son for these things, just as they honor the Father for these things!"

Now notice verse 30 also.

Again this is Jesus speaking,

"I can do nothing, on My own authority,"

"...as I hear, I judge, and My judgment is just, because I seek not My own will, but the fulfillment of the will of Him who sent Me!"

Verse 31,

"I do not have any witness of My own. I cannot bear witness to Myself!"

In verse 32 He says,

"...there is another who bears witness to Me, and I rely on His testimony, because I know that the testimony He bears to Me of Me is true,"

Can you see that we might as well add there,

"...therefore also, He bears witness of Me,

...He bears witness to Me, and to My ministry!"

"He acknowledges and recognizes and affirms, and approves Me; My ministry!"

Can you see how Jesus operated, not only in the legal aspect of righteousness, *but also, in the practical aspect of righteousness?*

He walked, in righteousness, and intimate fellowship with God!

He walked, in true relationship, deep intimate relationship and fellowship with God!

He listened!

He looked!

He grasped and understood!

He walked, in sensitive relationship with God!

He listened and looked!

He remained, in *sensitive fellowship* with God!

...sensitive fellowship with God ...sensitive friendship!

...And therefore He remained, in a place of sensitivity, to the Holy Spirit!

He walked, and remained, in that sensitivity!

That is what *abiding* is all about!

This is why, even Jesus, spent much time *in the presence of His Father,* talking to the Father, (which religion calls prayer,) but Jesus was communing with His Father in conversation, around the truth of Scripture and around life in general; the general happenings of his day, *conscious of the Father's most immediate nearness;* communing back and forth with His Father!

...enjoying Him, fellowshipping with Him.

He spent much time cultivating an intimate relationship with His Father, in the Holy Spirit, in the secret chamber, in the privacy of His heart, *even while in the midst of a crown, or while hanging out with friends.*

He learned to do that, *without being disconnected in His friendship and fellowship with His friends and those around Him.* He learned how to connect with both God and Man *intimately!*

He treasured intimate relationship with His Father, *enjoying Him, and fellowshipping with Him,* and therefore He found the time to be alone. In fact, He spent a lot of time with people *interacting and connecting,* but He also spent much time alone, in the secret place ...sometimes all night long,

...because there was too many distractions and demands of life and ministry, in the daytime.

And it wasn't a religious thing now, okay, some duty, and some obligation He had to perform!

"I must now go and spend all that time in prayer now, it's the source of my anointing!"

No!

Fulfilling some religious duty and obligation was not the source of His anointing!

He fellowshipped with God His Father all the time, *in His heart!*

He spent much time in His presence, and He loved being alone with Him!

He fellowshipped with His Father all the time, *in His heart,*

...*even in the midst of a crowd,*

...remaining sensitive in His heart,

...*having His inner ear open to His Father, to the Holy Spirit within Him,*

...and the eyes of His understanding open, His spiritual eyes open, amen.

He spent much time in that place of fellowship and prayer, *communicating back and forth, heart to heart, <u>not because of duty or obligation</u> but because of love!*

He was in love with His Father!

He enjoyed Spirit to spirit relationship,

...Spirit to spirit combined!

Oneness with His Father!

He was addicted to His spirit-identity, to His righteousness!

He was addicted to His Daddy's *fellowship and approval and acceptance and love!*

He was addicted to that intimate connection, *to that intimacy!*

You see if Jesus' anointing,

...and if Jesus' authority,

...was just mechanical,

...was just automatic,

...then He needn't have bothered cultivating His spirit-identity, and His relationship and fellowship with the Father!

163

…it wasn't a need anyway;

…it was the joy and rejoicing of His heart!

…He absolutely enjoyed it;

…He was addicted to that identity and that fellowship and that feedback and that friendship!

Righteousness was His life!

The truth of His spirit-identity was His life!

God was His life!

Fellowship with His Father was His life!

That intimacy was His life!

His very life!

You see Jesus didn't just wake up in the morning and walk in arrogance, and say,

"Well, you know, I am the righteousness of God, I'm the Son of God, where is the next demon, let Me have him, I'm going to cast this guy out!"

No listen, *He understood that He had to walk in absolute dependence,*

…yielding,

…submitting to God,

…all the time,

…withstanding the Devil,

…withstanding …and listening to God,

…listening…

Now don't receive that in a legalistic kind of a way now okay!

Jesus understood these things, *but it wasn't works to Him!*

Yes, it was essential for Him to do these things,

…but, it wasn't something He HAD to do!

…some duty, or obligation or something!

It was something He absolutely wanted to do, and enjoyed doing!

It was just who He was and is, *not something He was trying to live up to!*

He didn't have a pride and ego problem!

Humility isn't something He has to try and put on!

Humility is *who He is!*

There is no room for pride to co-exist with the Divine nature, *with love!*

Love and pride do not co-exist!

True humility in the spirit is about, *being in love!*

Being in love with your Daddy God!

Being in love with your righteousness!

Being in love with that image of yourself, the true you, *which God shows you!*

...I am referring to *that original design and true spirit identity of your being!*

...*that image and likeness of God on the inside of you!*

True spirit humility is being in love *with your true righteous self, and with God living on the inside of you!*

Truly understanding your righteousness does not make you self-centered and prideful and arrogant!

No!

Truly understanding the subject of righteousness;

...truly understanding your righteousness *makes you God inside minded!*

God abiding in you and you abiding in God!

"I in you, and you in Me!"

Jesus had no problem yielding and submitting to God!

He had no problem yielding and submitting to LOVE!

No!

Listen, He loved walking in absolute dependence upon His Father,

...upon His Father's Spirit within Him!

He loved yielding and submitting to His Father God!

Life was an adventure!

He enjoyed waking up and going on life's adventure with His Father!

It was easy to withstand the Devil!

...all the time, always!

He said,

"The Devil may be coming at Me, but he has nothing in Me!"

Jesus enjoyed and loved His fellowship with His Father, all the time!

He walked in that fellowship, all the time,

Not because He had to,

...but because He enjoyed it!

He enjoyed listening to His Father!

He enjoyed listening to His voice!

He loved listening!

Listening!

All the time!

There, in His inner man.

Right in the middle of life!

Right in the middle of a crooked and perverse generation, *among whom He shined as a light!*

He was a beacon of fellowship with God!

He was a beacon of life and love and inner peace and contentment and enjoyment!

He enjoyed God His Father!

He enjoyed life!

He enjoyed people!

He enjoyed life together with His Daddy God!

He enjoyed walking in the power of God!

168

He enjoyed walking in the love of God!

He enjoyed walking with God!

Walking in righteous relationship with God!

Jesus didn't do anything out of a sense of obligation, in His relationship with His Father.

Religion always emphasizes that sense of obligation.

It is one of the enemy's biggest tactics.

The minute you start thinking in terms of obligation, *you are now leaning on your own strength, to try and live up to that obligation,*

And then you immediately lose your sense of righteousness,

…you immediately lose your sense of joy and enjoyment,

…and you immediately lose your sense of innocence and so also your sense of intimacy,

…And the energy of God leaves you!

…The anointing leaves you,

…*it is no longer available to flow in!*

...And so love leaves you, and joy and enjoyment leaves you!

...And so now you're still trying to love people and minister to them, but it's no longer effortlessly flowing out of you; it becomes laborious,

...because you are no longer leaning on God,

...because you have stopped taping into your righteousness ...you have stopped taping into God's energy and power and love within you,

...and you have started relying on yourself again,

...on your own works and your own ability to love and your own efforts to try and please God!

It is a subtle thing, *but it will make you lose your sense of righteousness!*

It will drag you *right back into condemnation!*

The only way to keep flowing in the anointing is *to walk in a righteousness-consciousness* ...to maintain your innocence-consciousness!

...To walk in a love-consciousness!

...To walk enjoying that righteousness!

...enjoying that innocence,

...enjoying that intimate relationship and fellowship with your Father!

...And then everything flows from that fellowship and relationship!

...Ministry flows out of that!

...The anointing flows out of that!

So, Jesus walked in innocence.

Jesus walked, in sensitive relationship to God.

You see Jesus was tempted, in His thoughts, to go by what His think tank would suggest, *just like the rest of us!*

...but, He listened to His heart and He listened to God!

His link with eternal truth was never severed; *His ties with it remained unsevered.*

His relationship with God was *alive!*

He listened to God!

He walked in innocence with God!

He inclined His ear, to the word of God, to the truth revealed to Him, concerning Him, speaking to Him in the Scriptures, concerning Him; *concerning His identity and mission.*

...to see, to hear, to act, accordingly!

He listened to that voice of eternal truth alive within Him,

...and He listened to the voice of God quickened within Him, by the Holy Spirit of God, abiding within Him!

He walked *in sensitive fellowship with God,*

Thus, He walked in righteousness, and the anointing!

You see, that's what we'll have to do, too!

That's how we have to walk,

...in that same intimate sensitive fellowship!

Jesus did not just take for granted, that God said,

"This is My beloved Son, <u>in whom I'm well pleased</u>!"

The Father could have just said:

"This is My beloved Son,"

172

...and that would have been enough recognition and acceptance already.

...enough of an acknowledgment of the Sonship and identity of Jesus.

But you see, He already enjoyed that recognition and acceptance, and the approval that comes with it, all His life.

The mere knowledge of it was not enough for Him; for knowledge merely puffs up, He wasn't satisfied with mere knowledge. It went much deeper. He desired to live and walk in the full reality of His sonship.

You see, it became more than just doctrine to Him, more than just *"the doctrine of grace and identity."*

I mean, it is wonderful to **know** that I am My Daddy's Son and that I am accepted in the Beloved!

It is enough to enjoy that place of recognition and acceptance; **the knowledge of it!**

And Jesus had that, He had that all His life; He had that already from birth.

But you see, knowledge merely points to **reality.** And Jesus wanted **the full reality of it!**

...And the Father also could have just said,

"This is My beloved Son," and stopped there.

And for many, the mere knowledge of that, that simple recognition, would have been enough.

That would have been enough acceptances for some, enough recognition and approval of **positional** righteousness,

…and sad to say, but for many that is enough, they are satisfied with that knowledge, **with knowledge and doctrine alone,**

…but now notice, the Father didn't just say, *"This is My beloved Son,"* and stop there, no, He said,

"This is My beloved Son, **in whom I am well pleased!"**

You see, Jesus knew that God's pleasure in His life *was linked to His actual relationship and fellowship with His Father!*

You see He already walked for 30 years, *in righteous relationship with His Father,*

…enjoying that acceptance and that righteousness, and that innocence, and that deep intimate fellowship,

He already walked for 30 years, *resisting the Devil,*

He already walked for 30 years, *without sin; without embracing an inferior identity of*

Himself; without embracing an inferior relationship with His Father.

He already walked for 30 years, *resisting sin; wanting nothing to do with the lie and the inferior life it tries to sell him.*

Jesus already walked for 30 years, *without sin,*

…before that event ever happened,

…and that's why He received recognition from His Father publicly,

…*because He already received that recognition privately,*

…because He was not just already given recognition at birth,

…*but He personally received and fully embraced that recognition privately!*

That is why the Father said,

"This is My beloved Son, (and then He added) …in whom I'm well pleased!"

You see, I cannot afford to ignore God's recognition of my life, *and just take it for granted!*

I cannot be lax, or be casual, about my sonship; about my identity as a child of God,

...about being accepted in the Beloved and being welcomed in the Father's bosom,

I cannot be lax, or casual, about God's recognition of my life!

I cannot be flippant about these things!

You know, every human being wants to be recognized!

Every Human being wants to enjoy *real approval and acknowledgment.*

None of us like to be ignored, or to be shunned.

Every human being wants to be recognized!

...and people do the funniest things to be recognized,

...but I am telling you now, *the most important thing in life is to be recognized by God!*

Not just in the sense of, God loves me,

...and has declared me righteous, and has accepted me in the Beloved, in Jesus, and holds nothing against me,

...not just in the sense of, God reckons me legally righteous, because of the work of redemption,

...seeing me legally right,

...*but to know that, God reckons me vitally right,*

...*to know that, God reckons me His friend, and close companion,*

...*not just some estranged son of His!*

You see, I don't want you to misunderstand me now.

When God reckoned us righteous in Christ, and raised Him up, *because of our justification,*

...*because of our righteousness,*

...*because of us being made righteous,*

...that righteousness was *real*, amen,

...it is *vital*, amen,

...and it was given to us *as a gift,* amen,

...and so, there is nothing we can do, *to earn* that righteousness!

Religion is always trying to get you, *to earn,* what you already have!

You are as righteous as can be in your Father's presence!

Your Father loves you!

You are His precious child, and can refer to Him now as, ABBA, as Daddy!

He has made you accepted in the Beloved!

You are as innocent as can be in your Father's presence!

He reckons you totally totally righteous!

So what I am talking about, is not, questioning that righteousness, and putting it in jeopardy again,

...as if there are different levels of righteousness that can now be achieved,

...and here we go again, falling into works, and our own religious efforts, of prayer and fasting and repentance and what not,

...to try and get there!

To try and obtain, *what we already <u>have</u>!*

So I'm not saying that!

But I do want you to realize that there is an enormous difference between simply having access, *and actually entering in!*

There is a big difference between, just having access,

...but then, to actually enter in, making full use of that privilege, and that reality,

…enjoying to the fullest, that innocence, that wonderful intimate righteous relationship with Father God, with your lover,

…with your Daddy God!

Hey, Jesus didn't die for anything less!

…for a lesser reality, than the real deal!

What is fake is fake!

…and what is real is real!

God is not about to fool Himself!

He did not restore us to the fullness of our sonship, *so that we can again be wayward sons!*

Hey, Jesus died for more than that!

"Without faith, it is impossible to please Him."

But faith pleases Him!

…and in faith, it is possible to give Him pleasure.

"All those who come to God, must believe that He is, who He says He is, that He is love, and that they are, who He says they are, they are His kids, and accepted in His sight, and welcome in His presence!"

179

"They must understand, that He Himself, is the reward, and therefore also, the rewarder, of those who passionately love Him, and desire Him!" (Hebrews 11:6)

Listen this is not something you can *earn!*

It is not something you can *strive for!*

…or strive towards!

It is not something you can *achieve!*

It is only the portion of the pure in heart … *the ones who genuinely love God and is in love with Him!*

…the ones who do not come to play tit-for-tat games with God!

God wants a genuine intimate love-relationship!

He knows when you are in love, with *HIM,*

…and not with, what He can do for you!

Titus 1:15 & 16

"To the pure, all things are pure, but to the unbelieving and to the defiled, nothing is pure; their very minds, and consciences, are corrupted!"

"They profess to know God, but they deny Him, in their heart and therefore in their

deeds; they are detestable, disobedient, and unfit for any good deed!"

God is not fooled, by the ones who always do things, *with hidden motives, and hidden agendas!*

…You know, the ones who do everything right,

…but always expect something in return!

Only those, who receive, (those who fully embrace) the abundance of grace; the immense love of God for them; (who fully embrace) the gift of righteousness, of a fully reconciled, intimate, fellowship in relationship with God, *shall reign in life,* through the one, Christ Jesus!

If you make Him, *your exceedingly great reward,*

If you treasure your righteousness, and enjoy that righteousness, *and enjoy Him,*

…intimate friendship and fellowship with Him,

*…*He comes to abide within you, and make His home within you,

…and His very presence, and anointing, and reward, and favor, come with Him,

…to rest upon you, and abide within you!

Everything with God *is a gift!*

You can't earn anything, *as a reward!*

Not even through obedience, or duty and obligation!

It is the fruit of sweet intimate fellowship with Him!

...the fruit of a love-affair!

...and that intimate fellowship; that love-affair, is the fruit of the word of truth, embraced, and alive in your heart,

...it's the fruit of treasuring the truth of the gospel in your heart,

...letting the word of Christ, dwell in you <u>richly</u>,

...it's the fruit of that word of righteousness!

...that righteousness fully embraced and enjoyed!

Even our very obedience is a fruit of that!

...it's a fruit of the impact of the word upon our hearts,

...the impact of intimate fellowship with God, in the truth of the word!

So, everything with God *is a gift!*

It comes to you, by His working within you, both to will, and to do, of His good pleasure,

...holding fast the word of life!

Listen, you truly can't earn anything *as a reward,*

...His fullness is attached to His pleasure!

You are the joy and the rejoicing of His heart!

He is in love with you!

And when He, through revelation knowledge, *through the truth of the gospel,*

...through your total embrace of that righteousness,

...when He, becomes the joy and the rejoicing of your heart,

...and you fall head over heals in love with Him,

...then, there is chemistry,

...God's recognition is fully yours,

...and the anointing flows,

...and God acknowledges your life and ministry!

Now that is approval my friends *...the greatest approval and applause you can ever enjoy,*

...to be aware of, and to experience God's pleasure over you!

...to hear, and to intimately know, God's well done!

I pray that from now on, you too, will refuse to be flippant, to be casual, *about God's recognition of your life!*

I say again: **The most important recognition you can ever enjoy in life,** *is to be recognized by God!*

...because, that means, the highest level of authority is behind me,

...it backs me,

...He backs me, amen!

I mean, even in business, *if you can be recognized and endorsed, promoted even, by some large company ...and they recognize you as a tremendous young person, and they sponsor you for college, and gets behind you with some tremendous scholarship, or something ...I mean wouldn't that be something! To have all the finances and all the recognition behind you, I mean, you've got it made!*

Listen, you've only really got it made, *when you've got the Father's recognition!*

...when you've got His recognition in your heart

...and so, you'll also enjoy His recognition of your life!

So, Jesus had the recognition of His Father.

...And so Jesus' life was recognized by His Father!

Amen, hallelujah!

That is awesome!

What we are discovering together in this book is awesome, amen!

These are awesome things!

Chapter 7

The Importance Of Faith Gained Through Revelation!

So, *Jesus' life was recognized by His Father*,

...but what pleased God in His life?

What pleases God?

It's the obedience of Faith!

Faith pleases God!

Faith's obedience pleases God!

Jesus had to walk by faith!

Listen, Jesus had to walk in every principle of faith that you and I have to walk in!

And what is faith?

Faith is a sensitive relationship to the word;

...to the word of truth, to the truth of God revealed by God!

Therefore, faith is a sensitive relationship to the desire and will of God!

Listen, Isaiah 50:4 & 5 is not just a prophesy about the Messiah, which only applied to Jesus!

No, this is a prophetic instruction to us, the Church of the Lord Jesus Christ, **to all of God's sons and daughters,** *to be of the same mind, to have the mind of Christ!*

We read in Isaiah 50:4 & 5,

"Morning by morning, daily, constantly, He awakens my ear to hear,"

"...to be as those who are taught."

"The lord God has opened my ear,"

"...and I was not rebellious,"

"...I did not become backward in my thinking, and in my actions, and in my conduct!"

"Therefore the Lord God has given me the tongue of the learned, the tongue of the wise,"

"...the tongue of those who are taught of the Lord,"

"...that I may know, how to sustain, with the word, him that is weary, or worn out, in religion; in his own striving!"

Proverbs 4:1-15, and 18-26, gives a similar instruction,

"Hear, o sons, a father's instruction,"

*"...**and be attentive, that you may gain insight!***"

"For I give you good precepts **(or insights into truth)***:*"

*"...**do not forsake my teaching.**"*

*"When I was a son with my father, **tender**, the only one **in the sight of** my mother,"*

(...**when my heart was right *I was their favorite child!***)

"...he taught me, and said to me,"

'Let **your heart** <u>hold fast</u> *my words;'*

'*...keep* **(treasure)** *my commandments, and* **live;**'

(...**enjoy the pleasure it brings! Enjoy the life of it!**)

'*...**do not forget, and do not turn away** from the words of my mouth.*'

'**Get wisdom; get insight.***'

'**Do not forsake the truth, do not forsake that wisdom, and she will guard you.***'

'The beginning of wisdom is this: **Get wisdom, and whatever you get; get insight.**'

'**Prize her highly, and she will exalt you;**'

'…**she will honor you if you embrace her.**'

'**She will place on your head a fair garland;**'

'…**she will bestow on you a beautiful crown!**'

Verse 10 continues,

"Hear my son, and **accept** (or embrace) my words, **that the years of your life may be many.**"

"**I have taught you the way of wisdom;**"

"**I have led you in the path of righteousness.**"

"When you walk in it, **your steps will not be hampered;**"

"…and if you run with it, **you will not stumble!**"

"**Keep hold of that instruction, do not let go!**"

"…**guard the truth of your righteousness for she is your very life!**"

Now verse 14 & 15 says,

"Do not enter the path of the wicked, and do not walk in the way of evil men."

"Avoid that path, do not go on it!"

*"Turn away from it and **keep going with righteousness**"*

Verse 18 & 19 says,

"The path of the righteous winds ever upward,"

"It is also like the light of dawn, which shines brighter and brighter until full day, until the sun rules the day"

(…**or, until you, son, own the day and rule it!**)

"The way of the wicked on the other hand, is like deep darkness;"

"…they do not know, they do not realize, the treasure over which they stumble!"

Now verse 20 - 26,

*"My son, **be attentive** to my words;"*

*"…**incline your ear** to my sayings."*

"Let righteousness, let the truth not escape from your sight;"

"Keep that truth within your heart!"

"For it is life to him who finds it,"

"...and healing to all his flesh."

"Keep your heart focused on the truth and on your righteousness with all vigilance;"

"...for from it flow the springs of life!"

(...or from it flows the anointing!)

"Put away from you speech that does not line up with that reality of righteousness,"

"...and put all deviation from that truth far away from your conversation."

"Let your eyes be set,"

"...and let your single-minded gaze be established,"

"...and take heed to the path of your feet, then all your ways will be sure!"

Do you see how Jesus must have read these same scriptures, and how they came alive to Him, and how that Jesus Himself therefore *walked in every principle of faith* that you and I have to walk in!

He walked in a sensitive relationship to the word of God, to the word of truth, *to the truth of God revealed to Him by God Himself, in the Scriptures, through the Holy Spirit of Truth, abiding in Him!*

He walked in a sensitive relationship to the voice of God, *and to the desire and will of God!*

Jesus walked by faith!

He walked in his righteousness; He walked by the Spirit of wisdom and revelation in the knowledge of God, by insight and revelation into His spirit-identity, *and He yielded to it!*

He enjoyed His righteousness,

...He enjoyed His full identity and His right standing with God because of it,

...and that's why He pleased God!

Jesus walked by <u>that faith</u>, *and that's what pleased the Father!*

...because you have to hear in order to please God!

...you have to hear for there to be faith!

"...without faith it's impossible to please God!"

People, we need to see this!

Listen, I do not care how long you've been in ministry, *...ministry never ever becomes just automatic!*

I cannot afford, for even one day, to go on yesterday's manna, yesterday's food.

If the truth of God, if your righteousness *is not fresh to you,*

...if you do not appreciate it, and treasure it like you should, <u>on a daily basis</u>, moment by moment even,

...you will lose ground in your relationship with God,

...something so special, something so precious and valuable between you and God, *will begin to wane and die!*

...your love will begin to grow cold,

...you will lose your passion and your fire,

...and you'll lose something in the anointing!

...and the anointing may even stop flowing all together!

You see you might have seen mighty things happen a year ago, and the other day, and last week, and yesterday even,

...and you could have had an experience so powerful you can write books about, ...but if you don't daily walk in the principle aspect of righteousness, in the practical aspect of it,

...appreciating and walking in righteousness,

...in practical righteousness,

...enjoying that righteousness,

...and living that righteousness,

...then, in the spirit, you're nothing!

...you're nothing without God!

Unless God reckons me, *I'm nothing!*

With God I'm everything,

...but without intimate fellowship with God, I lose everything,

...and you see, the Devil immediately takes advantage of that!

Can you see how crucial it is, for us to operate in the authority *that is recognized by the Father?*

...the authority that righteousness alone can afford us!

Jesus walked and operated in the authority of His righteousness!

He walked in the authority that was recognized by the Father!

He walked in that authority of righteousness!

That is why He walked in the authority of the Father!

He said,

"I do not do anything on my own authority,"

...but His whole life was a reflection, and an exhibition, of the authority of God!

I read that again this morning in my morning devotions, **how they recognized Jesus' authority!**

Matthew 7:28 & 29

*"And when Jesus finished these sayings, **the crowds were astonished at His teaching,"***

*"...**for he taught them, as one who had authority, and not as their scribes.**"*

Remember also in Matthew 8:23-27, where it talks about Jesus sleeping in the boat, and how the winds and the waves came against them, and they woke Jesus up to deal with the situation.

It says, verse 26 & 27,

*"...Then He rose and rebuked the winds and the sea; and there was absolute calm. **And the men marveled, saying, 'What sort of***

man is this, that even winds and sea obey him?'"

Right after that event, we read in verse 28 - 34 *how the demons also recognized his authority,*

…and the story ends with the people actually getting filled with fear, *because of the display of that kind of authority and power.*

…they weren't sure who or what they were dealing with, *certainly not no ordinary man; it scared them greatly!*

You see, Jesus' authority was recognized by men, and His authority was recognized by the Devil!

Remember the little boy with the epilepsy?

Jesus spoke, and the demon manifested, and Jesus rebuked the thing and got rid of it, He cast it out, and He got that kid set free, *because of His authority!*

…but what does He say,

John 5: 30,

"I can do nothing on My own power"

"I am only yielding to the authority of the Father!"

He says in verse 19 & 20,

"Truly, truly, I say to you, the Son can do nothing of His own accord, but only what He (constantly, clearly) sees the Father doing;"

"...for whatever the Father does, that the Son does likewise."

"For the Father loves the Son, and shows Him all that He Himself is doing;"

"...and greater works than these will He show Him, that you may marvel!"

You see, He simply yielded to what the Father was doing through Him!

He followed the prompting of the Holy Spirit, and then became part of the audience!

He simply watched, and saw what God was doing through Him,

...and He became, very much, a part of what happened!

He daily yielded to the authority of God, so the authority of God can be displayed through His mouth, displayed through His life, displayed through His ministry as a man ...*to confirm the rulership of God,*

...and the rulership of righteousness,

...over the enemy.

I also read this morning, *how they recognized the authority of the early disciples, and how they were affected by the anointing,* there in Acts Chapter Two.

And also there in Acts Chapter Three and Four,

Acts 4:13 & 14,

"Now when they saw the boldness of Peter and John, and perceived that they were uneducated, common men,

"...ignorant and unlearned fishermen," another translation says,

"...when they saw that they were uneducated, common men, they marveled and wondered;"

"...and they recognized that they had been with Jesus."

"They also saw the man that had been healed standing there beside them,"

"...therefore they had nothing to say in opposition."

You see, they saw that authority, and it became difficult to come against that kind of authority,

...because they knew, they were now not just coming against mere men,

...they were now coming against God, in opposing these believers and what they have to say!

Oh, hallelujah! How awesome is that!?

Chapter 8

Righteousness By Faith; By The Revelation Of Truth!

It is particularly essential for us to understand, *where the Law of Identification originates from.*

It originates *from the seed!*

It comes from the seed, *whatever seed you entertain or embrace!*

Seed produces after its own kind!

Under that Law of Identification, if I sow a pumpkin seed, *I'm going to get a pumpkin fruit, with more pumpkin seeds inside it!*

The identity is in the seed! (Genesis 1:11).

And now, just to back up what we said there, *about the seed of Adam,* **that now contains that corruption of the Fall.**

I want you to notice this interesting Scripture over there in Genesis 5:3,

"When Adam had lived a hundred and thirty years, he became the father of a son, in his own likeness, after his image."

Did you catch that?

Adam produces, *after his own kind.*

He produced a son, no longer after God's image, but after his own fallen image,

...just like him!

Romans 5:12,

"Sin came into the world, through one Man, Adam, and death, through Sin, and so, death spread to all men ...because all men was introduced to Sin, and became sinners."

It is particularly interesting also then, to take a look at that reference to Abel, in Hebrews 11.

Abel received recognition from God.

Under the Adamic Covenant,

...now that was, before even the Abrahamic Covenant, or the Old Covenant of the Law,

...Abel received recognition.

On what basis?

On the basis of faith!

Because, you shall know the truth, *and the truth shall set you free!*

…because, just like the life of sin …just so, the life of God also comes in seed form!

Jesus said,

"My words are spirit and life!"

"You are already clean by the words I've spoken to you!"

"Father keep them by Your word,"

Which word?

"Your word is truth!"

*…in other words, **the truth** of the gospel!*

…original truth!

*…**the truth** that has been from the beginning!*

James 1:18

"Of His own will, He brought us forth, by the word of truth!"

Verse 21,

"…receive with meekness, the implanted word, which is able to save your souls!"

Peter talks there in the book of 1 Peter 1:22 & 23 about the fact that,

"…our souls have been purified, in obeying the truth, by our spirit, through the Spirit,"

He says,

"...having been born anew,"

"...not of corruptible seed, but of incorruptible, through the word of God, which lives and abides forever"

He goes on to say,

"Now this is the word, which by the gospel, was preached to you!"

John also says in 1 John 3:9

"No one born of God continues to commit sin; for God's seed remains in him, and he cannot continue in sin, because he is born of God's seed."

And so you see, there is an extremely fascinating prophetic picture, *linked to Abel's faith and his recognition from God,*

...it was written and revealed, *for our benefit.*

But unfortunately now, most of our recognized Christian movements today **have fallen into tremendous error on the topic of sin.**

...and so the purity of the Christian faith has been hijacked and polluted,

...and now Christianity has become its own religion of sorts.

...most Christians today, have fallen into this error, and it is such a trap, that sets you up for works, and for failure, under your own efforts.

...it turns Christianity into another Law of Moses!

The error they have fallen into, and are propagating, is that, sin is just a choice!

...and that salvation is also then, just a choice!

To think that Sin is not a something, I mean a power, or an invisible dominion of sorts,

...that came into this world, and invaded the human race,

...to think that sin is just a choice, is deception, and it is dangerous.

If sin was just a choice, then Jesus needn't have come, and then He also needn't have died!

Did you know that?

Paul says in 1 Corinthians 15:14 that, *"If Christ was not raised from the dead, our preaching is useless, and so also is your faith then."*

He then goes on to say in verse 17 that, *"If Christ was not raised from the dead, your faith* *would be futile, **and you would still be trapped in your sins.**"*

So then, neither sin, nor freedom from it, is just a matter of choice, *but a matter of faith.*

If sin was just a matter of choice for us now *after the fall,* then Jesus needn't have come and He needn't have died and be raised and elevated to heavenly places, as a man.

So, to sin or not to sin is not just a choice!

Because then, you can just *feel* right, and do the right thing, and be right.

I can then just choose to override and violate the law of gravity, and get away with it!

I mean, I can just choose then, to go against the Law of gravity, and I can then just hold this book I am writing, up in the air, out in front of me, *and I can then just hold it out, indefinitely, against the law of gravity.*

...but no, listen, there is a law involved, and you will quickly find out that, it is *a law,*

...it is called, the Law of Gravity!

And you see, there is a law involved also, when it comes to sin,

...and it is called, the Law of Sin and Death.

I can <u>will</u> what is right, but I can't do it!

I will find out that *I can't do it!*

You see sin is not a choice!

We need to see Sin, *for what it is;*

…**we need to see Sin,** *as a power,*

…*an invisible dominion or authority,*

…*which needs to be broken,*

…*and which only <u>the</u> truth of God, revealed, <u>as it is in Jesus</u>, can set us free from!*

You see, that power must be broken, by another Law, *a stronger Law,*

…*a stronger power,*

…*a stronger invisible dominion and authority!*

…It is called: *The Law of Faith!*

...**And that Law of Faith is directly connected to another** *stronger Law,*

…*a stronger power,*

…*a stronger invisible dominion and authority!*

...*the invisible dominion and authority of <u>eternal TRUTH, ultimate truth</u>, as God has* *known it from the beginning, and then also re-revealed it, in Christ Jesus!*

Look at it this way,

…In the Fall, yes, Adam's choice was involved, but, Satan and his strong deception, the power of it, was also involved,

…and so, the power of Sin came over the will of man.

But now I want you to see something, *and if you can see this,* it will profoundly bless you, and help you connect the dots,

…and you will never ever, fall into that trap again, of trying to be righteous,

…and trying to live free from sin,

…by your own willpower.

Now notice here, *this is how Abel's <u>faith</u> functioned.*

We'll start, by getting into the conversation that the Lord had with Cain.

Genesis 4:6

"The Lord said to Cain, 'Why are you angry, and why has your countenance fallen?'"

Isn't it compelling, that God could read his spirit in his face?

God could read him like a book.

He saw right through him.

God saw his spirit in his face!

I tell people often, when I ask them to do something *and I can see they are not really interested in doing it,*

I say to them,

"Your face is speaking to me!"

"...And if I don't see something else in your face, real soon, then I'm not going to be very happy, and I might have to start flogging you!"

And then they immediately start smiling, *just at the mere thought, of me trying to flog them,*

Ha… ha… ha…

They can see the headlines in the newspapers already,

"World's most loving pastor, finally snaps, and flogs disciple!"

Ha… ha… ha…

I know you're laughing, but seriously, it's like pulling teeth sometimes, to try and get some disciples *to serve others, rather than themselves.*

These days, people are so corrupted in their being, and in their thinking, by the greed of our society, and so preoccupied with it, *that they do not want to serve, simply out of love for God, no, they want to get compensated or paid for everything they do!*

They are not among us long however; us bunch of radicals who love Jesus, *before they start changing.*

Changed by His righteousness!

Changed by His love!

…I love it!

I thank God for the transforming power of the gospel!

Now where was I before I got so rudely interrupted by these funny things that come to mind, and so easily distract me?

Oh yes,

God saw Cain's spirit in his face!

Genesis 4:6,

"The Lord said to Cain, 'Why are you angry, and why has your countenance fallen?'"

Now notice this, this is particularly intriguing,

God said to Cain,

Verse 7,

"If you do well,"

I want you to notice, that God is *still* speaking to Man, *after the Fall.*

I also want you to notice God is speaking *to fallen Man here,* and He says,

"If you do well, will you not be accepted?"

What is the obvious answer?

Sure!

Of course!

Can you see the answer there in God's question?

"If you do well, will you not be accepted?"

What happened just a moment ago?

God accepted Abel's sacrifice!

...because it was the fruit of faith!

I mean, what was in that sacrifice?

211

Faith!

Besides the little animal, *there was faith in that sacrifice!*

Where did Abel get that faith from?

From hearing, and yielding, and being tentative to the word!

...you see, Abel had a sensitive relationship to the message of God, hidden in Adam's words.

You see Adam spoke!

Adam obviously told them in considerable detail, what happened in creation, *as far as he knew and understood.*

Obviously Adam told them, *of the bliss that was involved, and enjoyed, in intimate companionship with God!*

And obviously Adam told them, *of God's kindness, and His love!*

Obviously Adam told them, of God's mercy, because of love, and he told them of God's kindness; *what He did for Adam and Eve!*

Obviously, he told them,

'You know what God did?'

I can just see the emotion on Adam's countenance, *as he reminisces on these things, and as he is trying to tell them the story,*

...I mean, I can just see those little children as well, as they are sitting there around the camp fire, *hanging on his lips,*

...just hanging on every word,

...as they discovered where they come from,

'I mean, Dad, you mean to tell me, I don't just come from my mother's womb!'

'...but you mean to tell us that we all have a bigger beginning than our beginning here on planet earth, and that there is a Creator, who gives us all life!'

'...and from whom we really come!'

I could just see them listen, you know, and get caught up into it, as they listen to this marvelous magnificent account of Man's creation.

And they heard the whole thing, first hand!

I mean, it was like they were there when it happened!

And he told them, Adam told them.

And by the way, if you go and study in Genesis, you will soon discover that these guys lived quite a couple of years,

…and how that Adam got way up in age, and how many people actually knew Adam, and his sons, first hand.

So I am sure they all knew the creation account, in detail, **Enoch and Noah included,** and that is how it got passed down to us all!

And I can just picture how, after a while, Cain got caught up in his own life, and in this natural world, and he might have sat there at those camp fires, later on in years, *kind of just looking around, and board, hearing his dad tell the same old boring stories Cain remembered from early childhood, over and over again.*

So Cain was kind of distant you know,

…but Abel was sitting there, listening very intently.

And so, through Adam's stories, something came alive in Abel's little heart; *a desire was born, to know this Creator God, more intimately,*

…and he was listening very intently to those stories,

…listening, to see if he could not perhaps discover a key, **you know,**

214

…find a key that would unlock for him, the way back, into enjoying the presence and friendship of God!

And one day, as Adam was speaking, and he told them,

'You know guys, we lost something in that Garden, when we sinned, we lost something between us and God, and we could no longer enjoy His presence, like we used to'

…and I can just see the guilt-ridden tears running down his face, as he told them, with regret in his voice,

'We lost something, and we discovered that all of a sudden, we were naked. We were left naked by sin …that glory, and that enjoyment, our very righteousness, was stripped from us, by our sin, and we lost it!'

'You know, in our minds, in our thinking and reasoning and interaction with the Devil, and those thoughts he introduced to us in conversation, we lost something in our hearts and our minds, we lost something so precious, and we couldn't get it back, no matter how hard we tried; we just couldn't get it back – we couldn't get back what we lost!'

'…we eventually just drifted away from God!'

I can still see the tears in Adam's eyes, as he related to them,

'Man, we lost something that was worth more than anything else!'

'We lost that innocence, we lost transparency, we lost that beauty of fellowship and friendship with God without shame and without guilt.'

'We didn't know fear! We didn't know embarrassment! We knew who we were! We walked clothed in His glory! And we were just like God!'

'When I was walking in fellowship with God, it was like I was looking in a mirror! When I was looking at God, it was just like I was looking into that river over there, and I could see my own face's reflection, in the eyes of God!'

'We had such sweet fellowship, in love, and suddenly, the Devil came on the scene, and we lost it; we lost it all!'

...and Abel perked up, and now he was listening, with bated breath,

...listening, very intently,

...and his eyes began to sparkle, as he heard his father say,

216

'And you know, God is so kind, and He must still love us so much, do you know what God did?'

'He went against His nature and killed a little animal. God killed an innocent lamb, just to make a covering for us. He clothed our nakedness, He clothed us with the skin of that innocent animal, that day there in His presence!'

'...and He made a covenant with us that day, and He promised us that your mother's Seed, will one day, crush the Devil's head!'

Hey, can you see it with me, can you see in Adam's account of the events that took place after the Fall that **this is the first time where God in His grace began to enter into our darkness with us;** *into our confusion and lostness, by speaking the language of an inferior identity, the language of that inferiority complex of guilt, shame, and condemnation we received from the father of lies, and embraced as our own.*

...God, for the first time, spoke that fallen inferior law-language which is not in line with His knowledge of us, but in line with that other inferior knowledge we partook of from that other inferior tree.

...He entered into our darkness and confusion and lostness and spoke that same inferior language of punishment due; that language of sacrifices and scapegoats,

217

and judgment; that inferior temporary blood covenant language.

You see, by speaking an inferior law-language in line with our guilt, and shame and condemnation, *God was revealing in a mystery...*

(Note: It was only a mystery, because we could no longer speak the same language as God; that superior language, in line with the tree of life; in line with the knowledge of God; *with His eternal knowledge of us.*)

...By speaking the language of guilt and of punishment due, and of sacrifices and scapegoats and judgment averted, *God was revealing and hinting towards His ultimate plan, His permanent fix that would eventually in time be revealed and understood in full.*

God was revealing that in that one Seed to come, Jesus Christ, He would personally come to *subvert* that inferior religious conversation; that inferior sin language; that inferior law-language, *and reestablish* (not yet another inferior temporary blood covenant related to sin), but *the original eternal love covenant; that original agreement reached within the Godhead concerning Man; that original eternal love-language of God, in line with the eternal LOGOS; and in that original-language, the eternal language of God revealed, He would permanently restore unto us our original innocence and righteousness and romance, and it would then not just be available for a few brave souls, like Abel and Enoch, and the handful of other faith heroes mentioned in Hebrews 11, but it would then be available for everyone; the entire human race, every single one of us, to enter back into and enjoy!*

You see; the blood of Jesus is not the necessary price for sin.

I say again: **The blood of Jesus does not reveal the price or payment needed for our sins. No, the blood of Jesus reveals** *the price needed for our faith.*

The blood of Jesus reveals the extreme lengths God was willing to go to in His grace, the extent God was willing to go to in His eternal extravagant love for us, to reveal His eternal forgiveness of us, and to reestablish our eternal innocence, and our eternal righteousness, *in order to convince us of our eternal value and worth to Him still, in spite of the Fall.*

You see, Jesus by revealing the love of God for us to us, by the price He was willing to pay, *in shedding His own precious priceless blood,* came by that extravagant display of God's love, *to rescue our minds from the lies we had believed and embraced;* to rescue us from that inferiority complex produced by it, *and thus He came to rescue us from the inferior futile religious ways inherited from our forefathers.*

You see, the one Seed, Jesus, in His person, and in His successful reconciliation achievement *became the new and living way back to the garden, back to the tree of life. He, the very LOGOS of God, is our access, by the Spirit of wisdom and revelation released in Him and by Him; that very wisdom and revelation in the original knowledge of God.*

I say again: **Jesus' blood does not reveal the price necessary for sin; no,** *it reveals the extreme lengths God was willing to go to in the demonstration of His extravagant love for us,* **in order to reveal our extreme value and worth to Him still,** *in spite of the fall,* **and so to rescue our minds from the lies and deception we have partaken of, and embraced, believed and lived; I am referring to those strongholds that created our hell; those strongholds of guilt, shame, condemnation, and inferiority; that very darkness and hell of our own making and Satan's making, we found ourselves living in after the Fall.**

1 Corinthians 1:30 says, *"Of God are you in Christ, who has become unto us wisdom and revelation from above; our original righteousness restored; our complete*

sanctification; our entire redemption, rescue and restoration!"

Jesus Himself said in Matthew 16:18 that *"I will build my CHURCH* (I will restore the original identity of those who can see and comprehend what I am about to reveal and accomplish on the cross and in My resurrection and ascension.) *and the gates of HADES,* (the gates of HELL; the spiritual strongholds of lies and deception, of blindness and spiritual darkness, that HELLISH EXISTANCE, the fruit of the Fall,) *shall not prevail against them,* (against My CHURCH, against those who know and understood their original identity and place in God restored to them by Me!)*"*

So, if the gates of HELL shall not prevail against the CHURCH of the Lord Jesus Christ; *against the children of God,* then it clearly means that HELL is not a part of God's domain; not a part of His kingdom, but instead it is the very stronghold Satan came to established in the Fall, and maintain through the fruit of that other tree; that law-tree; that inferior identity and inferiority complex tree; *that other knowledge, other than the knowledge of God.*

Thus, that HELL is strengthened through an inferior identity, and a focus on sin. That HELL is strengthened and reinforced through an inferiority complex of guilt, shame and condemnation.

It is that very HELL which Jesus said shall not prevail against His EKKLESIA, His CHURCH – *those who see and understand who they are as children of God, because of what God Himself revealed and restored to them in Jesus Christ.*

...And I am not saying there isn't another kind of HELL as a well, a very similar and yet different kind of HELL that awaits some people when they go through death's door and suddenly find themselves in eternity, *in that eternal spirit-dimension.* But as I was saying before, you should get my Study Course on the *"Gospel In 3-D!"* where I expound in greater detail about that.

But let's get back to Adam's camp-fire stories which he and Eve must have passed on to Cain and Abel, and all the rest of their children.

Now where was I? Okay, now I remember: So, there they all were, and Abel was listening very intently as Adam in vivid detail told their story ...how he remembered it.

...And Adam said,

'You know guys, we lost something in that Garden, when we sinned, we lost something between us and God, and we could no longer enjoy His presence, like we used to. We lost something, and we discovered that all of a sudden, we were naked. We were left naked by sin ...that glory, and that enjoyment, our very
222

righteousness, was stripped from us, by our sin, and we lost it!'

'...In our minds, in our thinking and reasoning and interaction with the Devil, and those thoughts he introduced to us in conversation, we lost something in our hearts and our minds, we lost something so precious, and we couldn't get it back, no matter how hard we tried; we just couldn't get it back – we couldn't get back what we lost!'

'...And so we were trapped in Satan's snare, and it all just became such a big nightmare, such a hellish experience ...and in the midst of all of that, and perhaps because of it, **we eventually just drifted away from God!'**

'...Because we couldn't face Him anymore, you see; we just couldn't face Him, and we no longer had that intimate connection, that intimacy we once had ...and so we just drifted away form God.'

And as I said before, I can almost see the tears in Adam's eyes, and hear the regret and remorse in his voice, the guilt and shame and condemnation and inferiority, as he continued relating to them, him and Eve's story,

'Man, we lost something that was worth more than anything else!'

'We lost that innocence, we lost transparency, we lost that beauty of fellowship and friendship with God without shame and without guilt.'

'We didn't know fear! We didn't know embarrassment! We knew who we were! We walked clothed in His glory! And we were just like God!'

'When I was walking in fellowship with God, I knew real peace! When I was walking with God, it was like I was looking in a mirror! When I was looking at God, it was just like I was looking into a peaceful reflection pool, and I could see my own face's reflection there, in the eyes of God!'

'We had such sweet fellowship, in love ...but then suddenly, the Devil came on the scene, and we lost it; we lost our inner peace; and we found nothing but turmoil, and in that turmoil and upheaval of our whole existence we lost it all!'

*...but it was at this point in the same old story they must have heard many many times that Abel perked up, **and this time he was listening with bated breath,***

...listening, very intently,

...listening with ears wide open,

*...**and his eyes began to sparkle,** as he heard his father say, '**And you know, God is***

224

*so kind, and He must still love us so much,
for do you know what God did and said?'*

*'God killed an innocent lamb, just to make a
covering for us. He clothed our nakedness,
He clothed us with the skin of that innocent
animal, that day there in His presence!'*

*'...and He made a covenant with us that
day, and He promised us that your mother's
Seed, will one day, crush the Devil's head!'*

...and Abel started thinking to himself,

*'Surely, if God covered their nakedness,
with the skin of that innocent young animal,
in His presence, if God made a <u>covenant</u>
with them, based on that blood sacrifice,'*

'...then, maybe <u>that's</u> my way in!'

*'...then maybe He will cover also my
nakedness, and receive me, and accept me,
<u>on that same basis</u>!'*

*'...on the basis, of that same blood
covenant, He established'*

...and, as revelation dawned on him,

...faith came alive, that day, in Abel!

Can you see how **God clothed them,** there in
the Garden, with the skin of that innocent
young animal?

Just as a side note here: **Humanity is tailor-made for God!** He clothed Himself in our skin when He brought us forth from within Himself to express His image and likeness in this natural dimension! Also, we were meant to be clothed with Him, with His presence; nothing else can clothe our spirit-man! I say again: **Humanity is tailor-made for God;** we were never meant to wear some other inferior covering, and clothe ourselves with something insufficient to properly clothe us *and keep us from being naked and exposed and vulnerable to the elements and whatever comes along to do us harm!*

...And, do you see also with me that God did not clothe Adam and Eve with skin, *because of some kind of Divine need to be appeased,* **but because of their unconditional love for Adam and Eve; for us?!**

The Godhead spoke the language of Adam and Eve's own judgment: **Adam, not God, was embarrassed about his nakedness.**

That clothing, that temporary blood covenant, *was not to make God look at Adam and Eve differently,* **but to make them feel better about themselves!**

...And ultimately *it was to prepare them, to prepare humanity, for the ultimate unveiling of the mystery of* **mankind's redemption in the incarnation.**

You see, it would be in the incarnation where **Deity would come and clothe themselves in human skin, in a Son, a son of Man, and in that person, in that man, in that son, the very Lion of Judah would become the Lamb of God, who would take away the sin of the world forever,** *and remove Sin out of the equation altogether,* **in order to free our minds from the lies we have believed and lived,** *so we may re-discover His image and likeness in our skin!*

Can you see that?

Can you see that God did not clothe Adam and Eve with skin *because of a Divine need to be appeased?*

Can you see that *that clothing was not to make God look at them differently,* but to *make them feel better about themselves?*

God did that *because of His unconditional love for Adam and Eve, for the human race; for us,* <u>*for you and for me*</u>!

And can you also see that **even when He put them out of the Garden,** *it was because of love – to protect them!*

He said,

"Lest they eat also now of the tree of life, and live forever"

(…living forever in this fallen state …lest they think they are confirmed in their error, still accepted and approved in this fallen state. I don't want them to get the wrong message *that I am now approving of* **this fallen inferior existence; of this HELL of their own making and Satan's making <u>which only results in self-destruction</u>**.)

...Now, hey listen, before they could be clothed with that skin of that innocent young animal God clothed them with, and covered their nakedness with, *that animal had to die,*

…there had to be the sacrifice of that young innocent animal's life!

It was an innocent substitute that stood in their place of punishment!

...**And in that, can you see how God was now speaking our inferior law-language,** *prophetically pointing to the one Seed that was to come, Jesus the Christ, who would come to our rescue, and become our eternal Savior?*

You know, **if judgment was in God's heart,** *if it was part of the agenda,* **if it was something He desired and was planning on doing,** God could and would have judged them right then and there; *He could and would have killed them for their high treason and betrayal, when they sinned,*

…I mean, He could and would have done it, *He would have gone ahead and punished them,* **but He didn't!**

God had legal right to wipe out the human race, right there in its beginning, right there, *but He didn't!*

He said,

"You'll surely die!"

…and they died, amen,

…but God didn't kill them!

…No, they died when they listened to the Devil, and then afterward, ate of that tree

…so, they were poisoned by the lie, by the fruit of that deception, and they died!

They died, spiritually!

…They died, in their relationship with God; in their fellowship with Him.

…They died, in their intimacy with Him!

…They died, as far as their deep intimate romance and love relationship, as far as their love-affair with God is concerned!

As far as a close intimate fellowship with God is concerned, *their fellowship ceased to exist!*

...And thus, they ceased to exist!

...They awakened to the power of the lie; they awakened to the deception, and to its HELL, and they ceased to exist as far as the possibility of again having *a real genuine deep friendship and fellowship with God* is concerned.

That fellowship between them and God, *the quality they once enjoyed, ceased to exist,*

...it died, amen.

But, God didn't kill them!

It wasn't God who killed them, amen!

Instead, He met them where they were at, and He joined them in their darkness and confusion and s*poke an inferior law-language out of necessity, a language in line with the Fall; a language they can relate to, and He gave them what they needed; He gave them a prophetic picture, by killing a young innocent animal!*

That young innocent animal paid an enormous price!

It paid with its life!

And through the death of that young innocent animal, *God communicated with them, in inferior picture language and parables, and He temporarily clothed Man!*

230

And you know what other compelling thing God showed me about that?

The first death occurred when Adam sinned, *and then came the second death,*

...the death of that young innocent animal, was the second death,

...prophetically, pointing to Adam's second death, in Jesus!

...prophetically, pointing to Jesus, and our joint death in Him, in which we co-died!

That blood was spilled, *and so we had the first inferior prophetic temporary blood covenant, pointing to Jesus!*

He, the promised Seed, the Seed of the woman,

He would come in the fullness of time, *to permanently, clothe us again!*

...To clothe us thoroughly, with the very eternal substance of the kind of love and truth His blood sacrifice communicates, *and thus, to clothe us with His very own robe of righteousness,*

...and restore again to us, our original righteousness, our original innocence,

...and our enjoyment and intimate fellowship with God in His bosom ...in total oneness with Him!

And you see, **Abel picked that little prophetic detail up**, *in the spirit,*

...with a sensitive ear, Abel picked it up!

You see, **faith was born, in that young man's heart!**

He felt like he was born anew,

He was brimming with joy and excitement,

...and I can just see him, smiling from ear to ear,

...because he finally grasped something of value, he grasped the way back in; the way back into fellowship, and approval, and intimate friendship and even romance with God!

...oh, I can just see how empty he was, how his heart was yearning after God, living in that hell of separation, yearning after the love of God; after God Himself, after God's very Person

...but now he was no longer seeking, he was no longer yearning, now his heart was burning with excitement to finally be able to escape hell altogether!

...his heart was burning with passion, to encounter God, and cultivate a friendship and love-affair with God!

You see, he used to lay awake at night,

...and think to himself, *'I wonder how I can approach God'* **He was wondering, how he can approach a God, *who still loved Man, but is no longer pleased with Man.***

Until he discovered, *faith,*

...through the words of his mom and dad.

You see, only *faith* can please God!

...and he began to believe,

...based on what he heard,

He began to believe that,

'Man, I can approach God; I no longer have to be afraid!'

'...I'll approach Him in faith!'

'...I'll approach Him, the same way He indicated for us to approach Him!'

'...on the basis, of that Covenant <u>He</u> made!'

'...on the basis, of that blood covenant!'

'...man, I used to wonder how I can even approach God,'

'…How can I approach a God, who perhaps might still love me; who perhaps might still love Man, but who is no longer pleased with Man?'

'…but now I have discovered, I can approach Him, I can approach Him by faith.'

'Faith pleases Him.'

'…and if faith pleases Him, then I can please Him again!'

'I can please Him again!'

Abel discovered righteousness by faith!

…and so did Seth, the brother that was born after his murder …probably by hearing the story of how Abel received recognition from God before his murder!

…So, Seth also discovered righteousness by faith, who then passed it on to Enoch, who then passed it on to Lamech, who in turn passed it on to Noah!

…and therefore it is said about Enoch that he too walked with God. He walked with God and was no more, for God loved him so much, He pleased God so much, that God took him!

Can you see how that story about Enoch, could only in the light of righteousness by

*faith possibly even make any sense, after
the Fall happened?!*

*Thus, it says, Enoch walked with God. He
just got plain raptured and caught up in his
relationship and love-affair with God ...and
then suddenly went home to Heaven; his
physical body being swallowed up and
dissolved and replaced by his eternal
immortal spirit-body! And thus, Enoch
walked with God, and could not be seen
anymore, and was nowhere to be found in
this natural dimension we live in, for God
took him into Himself!* (Genesis 5:24)

*...And thus, Enoch then also became yet
another prophetic picture of the man, Jesus
Christ, taken up bodily into the heavenlies,
absorbed into that realm of spirit reality,
and seated at and in the right hand of God
the Father, representing, in His person, our
eternal welcome there in that place, in the
bosom of the Father, forever!*

Hallelujah!

**There is a man seated, as, and in, and at,
the right hand of God!**

**By faith these men of old, like Abel and
Enoch,** *received Divine approval!*

Hebrews 11:1-6 says,

"Now, faith, is the substance (the reality) *of
things hoped for, the evidence* (the

revelation or insight into; it's the conviction of the existence of, it's the persuasion of, it's the reality) **of things not seen,"**

"For, by it, the men of old *(embraced, and)* **received Divine approval."**

And then it says,

"By faith, Abel offered to God, a more acceptable sacrifice than Cain, through which, he received approval,

...in regards to righteousness,"

"God bearing witness *(to that righteousness still available by faith)* **by accepting his gift;"**

"...he died *(physically)*, **but through his faith, he is still speaking** *(concerning the fact that righteousness by faith is still available, to the pure in heart, to those who want an intimate love relationship with God, in spite of the Fall)."*

Abel's faith, still speaks to us, concerning those things, amen!

...And thus he also became another prophetic picture pointing to Jesus; **to His sufferings as our Messiah,** *and to the subsequent glories that would follow the cross!*

Hebrews 11:5 goes on to say,

"By faith *(by having the same heart as Abel, and entering into this righteousness by faith)*

Enoch was (caught up in this truth, enjoying and partaking of the reality of it, **to such a degree** that he was) **taken up, so that he was not found, because God had taken him.**"

"**Now, before he was taken, he was also attested to, just like Abel, as having pleased God!**"

Verse 6,

"**For, without faith** (without believing that righteousness is still intact, and available, and without fully embracing and entering into that righteousness by faith) **it is impossible to please Him.**"

"**For, whoever would draw near to God, must believe that He exists, and that He rewards those, who <u>truly</u> seek Him.**"

"**They must first be convinced that He is whom He says He is; that He is love,**"

"...**and that they are, who <u>He</u> says they are, they are His kids, and accepted in His sight, and welcome in His presence!**"

"**They must understand that <u>He Himself</u> is the reward**"

"...**and therefore** (because of fellowship with Him, because of His presence, He is) **also the rewarder, of those, who passionately love Him, and desire Him!**"

You see, Abel listened to his dad's stories, and heard of how, even when God confronted Adam and Eve, *God made the Devil the culprit, and refused to judge, Adam and Eve* …**but instead, chose to clothe them in His presence, with the skin of an animal,** *not to make God somehow feel differently about them, but to make them feel better about themselves!*

…and, even though God had to put them out of the Garden, **to further protect them,** *He didn't destroy the Garden, or shut it with massive gates, and locked it up forever.*

…no, instead, He placed two angels at the entrance of the Garden, with two flaming swords.

...And Abel picked up on that significance too.

He picked up on the fact, that the way back in, *is hidden,* **but still available!**

It may even be hidden in these accounts somewhere; (in these historic references and stories told by his parents) *hidden there,* **for him to find.**

He thought to himself,

'There must be a key. And that key must be found, through my passion, and it must be found through insight and revelation. That key must be a hidden wisdom, into the mystery of God; and if I pay attention, and listen carefully

to my parent's stories, it will be revealed to me, and I will find it!'

So, Abel listened, and heard, and it struck him that that sacrifice that was made, the life of that young innocent animal, and the skin that was used to clothe his parents in the presence of God, *must be the key.*

Everything God did, indicated to him that there was still a way back in.

He even recognized that God gave Adam and Eve, a promise; *that the Seed of the woman will crush the head of the serpent!*

And even today still, in the eastern mind, *the head always speaks of the seat of government!*

The authority, the position of authority, the might, the power, the rule, and government of the enemy, *get's broken, through the Seed of the woman.*

God promised it, *and declared it!*

And Abel thought,

'Well, I was born of a woman, I could be that Seed to come. I will crush Satan's head, his rule over my own life, maybe not in my brother's, but surely in mine. I want my righteousness and authority restored. I want intimate relationship with my God restored.'

He thought to himself,

'I will use that same symbol, that same sacrifice, even that same animal, a young innocent one, of that same kind of animal, and I will approach God with it, and if I am right about this, He will accept me still, and then I will become that Seed that crushes Satan's head!'

'God will strengthen me, so that I won't have to submit anymore, to Sin, and to that Devil.'

'I believe, I can have my righteousness fully restored!'

'I don't have to live, trapped in an inferior identity; I can live free from the impact of the Fall, even after the Fall occurred'

'…by faith in God, I can!'

'Nothing is impossible to God!'

'I am convinced, by what I've heard, and understood, that Righteousness by faith is possible!'

Abel thought to himself,

'God could have killed my Dad, He could have killed my mother, but instead He killed a young innocent animal, and used the skin of the animal to clothe my dad, to clothe my Mom. He killed that young innocent animal, and used the skin to clothe my parents.'

And Abel was sensitive enough, hungry enough in his heart, *and he paid close enough attention, to pick up on God's symbols,*

…on God's indication, that the way into righteousness, and intimate fellowship with God was still open.

Abel was sensitive enough, *to see* the significance of what God did, *and what God was saying, in what He did,*

…and that's what afforded him revelation,

…God saw Abel's heart, and by His Spirit, granted Abel access again, through those two angels guarding Paradise,

…He granted him access, <u>to that treasure</u>, the two angels were guarding, "

…that treasure is called, *"The Tree of Life;"* it's called: *"righteousness by faith."*

…God granted Abel access, to that treasure, through those two angles: *The spirit of wisdom and revelation, in the knowledge of Him.*

Abel gained access, by those two angels, *by the spirit of wisdom and revelation, into the knowledge of God; he gained access into the real Garden and tree of life; the spiritual garden of fellowship; that Paradise!*

...*God by His Spirit, granted Abel that necessary revelation and insight, into words, into the Word of God, into the truth behind the stories of his father, Adam,*

...*and faith was quickened, and given birth to, in Abel's spirit; in Abel's heart,*

...*because of the purity of the desire of his heart;*

...*because he hungered and thirsted after righteousness!*

I am sure he got so excited by what he saw and understood that he immediately told his mom and dad,

*'Hey, you guys, stop crying over spilt milk, **the way into God's most intimate presence is still available!***'

But I can just see old Adam, with his inferiority complex, under that cloud of condemnation, shaking his head and saying,

'No, no, no, it can't be, it just can't be Abel, you are wrong son, I don't want to hear that foolish talk anymore. That is just wishful thinking! That is just arrogance! What you are saying is nonsense. It is just too good to be true. Son, I just can't get myself to believe it!'

...now maybe Adam believed again after the death of Abel,

…and after the whole story of God's approval of Abel, and God's acceptance of Abel's sacrifice finally came out …the Scriptures are silent on that matter and do not say anything further about it, but I would like to believe that it happened, that Adam also finally began to live by faith again!

...Even if that never happened, we know at least, that Abel's story did get out, **because it is recorded in the Scriptures,** so there is always a possibility of what I had pictured about Adam could have happened.

Listen, all the old patriarchs lived by faith!

Just as Hebrews11 says they did!

They entered into the same righteousness we enjoy, *by the same faith!*

They kept looking forward towards the coming Messiah, who would come and do an exchange of equal value and release them of all their sins, and they were able, by faith, to keep receiving a cleansing of their conscience, when they blew it, so that they may continue to walk with God.

It was a faith walk!

It was a faith issue!

They believed what Abel believed,

…they believed they were temporarily covered, on the basis of the blood covenant, on the basis of God's covenant with fallen Man, with Adam, and with them, *on the basis of God's promise!*

…and they kept looking away from the present, into the future, *unto Jesus who was to come!*

Looking forward, in faith!

We on the other hand, to some degree, also have to believe what Abel believed, *in order to enter into righteousness by faith,*

…they believed their sins were temporarily covered, and they kept looking forward, to Jesus,

…we believe our sins were completely forgiven, and Sin itself was dealt with, *and we enter into that freedom, by faith.*

…You see, we also have to look to Jesus, just like they had to, we look away from the present, but we look back, in faith!

...We see through the eyes of faith, and we understand what He did; *what He both revealed and accomplished!*

Jesus accomplished **our total reconciliation!**

You see, we look away, from the present, from ourselves, from the natural, from our natural identity, **unto truth revealed, unto salvation** established, unto redemption realities, unto Jesus, the Author and Finisher of our faith!

He is God's measure of our lives on full display!

Our lives are hidden with Christ in God!

He is the mirror, in which we clearly see our original design, *re-revealed, and redeemed.*

...We see *our true identity,* as sons of God, on display, there in Him,

...and we see, our total salvation and restoration, *accomplished, and revealed, there in Him!*

As long as He is seated, as a man, **at** the right hand of God, **as** the right hand of God, and **in** the right hand of God, *these things are a permanent eternal* **reality,**

...for us to embrace and experience and enjoy!

You see, from beginning to end, **life is a faith issue!**

Whether it was the patriarchs of old, or us for that matter; *the just shall live by faith!*

You see, faith is not of the mind, *it is of the spirit!*

It's not up there, in your top 5 inches; *it is at the core of your being; it is a living thing in your heart!*

And so, if Abel's faith pleased God, *then there must have been faith,* **in the heart of that young man!**

Now I want us to imagine his faith.

I want us to clearly see his faith, *because his faith still speaks!*

…**it speaks to us!**

…**and it tells us exactly what it told him!**

You see faith *is a living thing!*

…*and it can be imparted!*

And I want Abel's faith, *to speak to us right now,*

…*to be imparted to us!*

…*through these words I am writing!*

Abel, by faith, saw the prophetic significance.

Abel's faith was sensitive enough, to pick that up,

…to discover what God was indicating, and pointing towards,

…and to pick up, what God was saying.

Abel saw that **covenant!**

He saw that God had made **a covenant,** in what He did!

You see covenant has to do with *acceptance, recognition, and approval.*

The bottom line of relationship is *recognition.*

In a marriage covenant, that is what it's all about; *recognition, and respect of each other, as a person.*

…it's within that recognition that acceptance comes,

…it's within that recognition that relationship, and equality, are born,

…and respect and mutual agreement and approval come.

…and *this* was the hearts cry of this young man, Abel.

He wanted recognition,

…he wanted relationship restored,

…he wanted covenant relationship with His Maker, with His true Father; with His God!

And do you know what he did?

…his whole life was driven by that desire.

He took that revelation he received,

…and he began to raise those animals, not just any kind of animals, no, *the exact ones God used the skin of, to clothe his parents with in His presence.*

…Abel raised those animals, *because they spoke to him of a way back into relationship with God* …**that was his connection to God's symbol, and God's indication of a possible covenant relationship with Man,** *even after the Fall.*

And so you know what Abel did?

*…and I want you to see **the posture of his heart!***

He took his best, the best little young innocent animal in his herd that he could find, and he killed that little animal,

…and he built an altar, as a sign to God, that he is raising up and exalting God's own sign, God's own indication of these things, God's own symbol for **covenant.**

…he put that offering on that altar, as a sign to God, as a sign of respect to God, *exalting God's opinion, God's own symbol of the possibility of intimate friendship still,*

...so God could intelligently read his heart, and know what he was trying to say, as best he knew how,

...and he sacrificed that young innocent animal, and set it on fire upon that altar, *indicating his raw passion, his faith, his total persuasion about this before God,*

...indicating the passion and desire burning in his heart, for total innocence and righteousness by faith,

...for intimate covenant friendship with God!

...where, everything that is his is God's, and where, everything that is God's, is his.

That's what covenant friendship is all about!

It is mutual living!

A total sharing of one another's lives!

It speaks of *complete oneness!*

He approached God in that manner,

...he approached Him, by faith.

He was totally persuaded of these things.

He believed that there indeed was a God.

That God hadn't died or gone missing, or moved to the other side of the universe.

He believed that God was still, right there, **out of sight to the natural eye,** *but still very much in reach, and actually present.*

So he approached God.

He believed that there was a God!

He believed that God was!

He believed that God was!

God was a total reality to him!

Abel knew that they fell, *and that it was a reality,*

…but he also knew that God was, *and that* **God was a greater reality!**

*…***and he became so convinced!**

*…***and there was faith in his sacrifice!**

*…***his sacrifice was full of persuasion and conviction of the reality of these things!**

You see, faith is the substance, **the assurance** of things **hoped for.**

…and Abel was hoping, he was hoping, *that God would recognize the symbol, that God would recognize* **covenant,** *that God would* *recognize an approach* **according to covenant,** *that God would recognize* **faith;** **that God would confirm it; that God would confirm his faith,**

...that God would recognize him, and acknowledge him,

...and approve somehow, of that sacrifice,

...and approve somehow, of his faith,

...and confirm his faith **...and approve of him, and accept him,**

...and welcome him, and embrace him, into intimate covenant friendship and fellowship.

And so he came *with faith,* and with the blood of that young innocent animal,

...and the smoke of the sacrifice went up, and came to the nostrils of God,

...and God recognized his faith; *and acknowledged and confirmed his faith!*

God didn't recognize the dead animal; He didn't recognize the killing of animals, **so as to now condone animal sacrifices in worship, no,** *it wasn't about the animal.*

God recognized *the faith* **of this beautiful young man!**

…because God's heart already yearned for this young man!

Listen, God's heart *never changed* in spite of the Fall!

The heart of God *cannot change!*

God knows who you are!

His heart yearns after you!

He is in love with you!

He is crazy about you!

Did you know that that heart of God towards us *can even change God's mind?*

In Hosea 11, God spoke out His judgment in frustration against Israel, His people,

…but then He says,

"My heart recoils within Me!"

"I will not execute My fierce anger!"

…and so, **God's heart changed His mind!**

And so you see, even in the Fall, even in spite of the Fall, *God never changes His heart.*

His heart was still for intimate companionship with Man.

His heart was still for intimate fellowship with Man.

And so, when God's heart saw the heart of Abel,

...when God saw the expression of his faith,

...coming before God, with a faith sacrifice, approaching Him,

...perhaps speaking to God, either in his heart, or out loud, it doesn't matter,

...but I'm sure he must have said something like,

'God, who brought forth my father Adam and my mother Eve, from within Yourself, the very God who created me, who gave my spirit birth, and gave me life, the God from whom I came, God, I bring You this sacrifice, as a sign of my faith, it is my faith speaking God! God, I am approaching You, and speaking to You, because I believe that You are! Confirm my faith! Accept me please God!'

...and he received recognition!

God recognized Abel's sacrifice; *Abel's heart, <u>his faith</u>,*

...and He confirmed Abel's faith and gave Abel approval, and recognition,

Abel received recognition from God,

…and God reckoned him righteous!

…because of his faith!

You see, life is not a snakes and ladders game ("Shoots & Ladders" in the USA) **where the fall of the dice dictates! No, we begin at the FINISH line! Life begins at *"IT IS FINISHED!"* Faith begins at the ULTIMATE CONCLUSION!**

When FAITH is born Deuteronomy 28 becomes obsolete!

I say again: **In a FAITH environment, in FAITH's conclusion, Deuteronomy 28 is outdated! *We are no longer chasing blessings and dodging curses!***

Every blessing heaven has was already lavished upon us <u>from the beginning</u>, *and therefore re-revealed in the fullness of time; it was <u>thus</u> re-lavished upon us in Christ* (Ephesians 1:3-4).

And every definition of curse, even the idea of it, was also therefore forever canceled and reversed on the cross! (Galatians 3:13).

You see, we are designed to participate in our divine origin, *simply by reflecting, and discovering,* not striving.

We must all learn to rest in the effortlessness of reflection, *so we may learn to speak God's language of romance and enter into it!*

That's how Abel's faith worked, *and thus he discovered his way back into the garden, back to the tree of life!*

You see, if BELIEVING isn't effortlessly based on eternal truth we have discovered, *then it's merely "make belief!"*

Faith is easy, *it's based on a correct conclusion in the ultimate truth; eternal truth.*

Faith is merely the <u>fruit</u> of insight and revelation into that truth!

Many people interpret, *"to walk by faith and not sight"* as very difficult; a very difficult, almost unnatural walk; *yet it is the very mode of our being! It's our very design!* We are wired to BELIEVE, especially when ultimate TRUTH is revealed!

Believing is like breathing! If believing had to be the reward of my own diligent study, *instead of a gift freely given by God's Holy Spirit of wisdom and revelation in the knowledge of Him* ...if breathing had to be the reward for my diligent study of how the lungs function, *and then my constant conscious application and concentration,* then we would override the ability of our design to breathe naturally and freely!

The Christ-life is the life of our design; therefore the faith-life is also the life of our design! But I thank God for the manifold, multifaceted expression that God has in each and every unique individual – each and every one of us! When we realize this, competition goes out the door! There is no such thing as competition in a faith environment! No one can replace you! For, no one can replace the uniqueness of you; your distinctness!

Paul writes in 2 Corinthians 10:12, that while we do compare ourselves with one another and thus compete with one another, *it is only proof that we are STILL without understanding!*

Hey, we are not merely Christ-cloned, we are individually uniquely and awesomely designed *to give full display to the image and likeness of our Maker* within our own unique individual personality, our fingerprint, our touch, our smile, our voice, our countenance!

All of that only functions best within an environment of faith!

Paul says, we do not preach ourselves, we preach Christ (we preach our original design, and our full redemption and reconciliation in

Him), **therefore we commend ourselves to everyone's conscience!**

He says in another translation, we do not preach ourselves, we preach Christ, yet we recommend ourselves (that original design on display in us) **to everyone's conscience!**

...Thus, by faith, Abel too *received recognition from God!*

...Abel was recognized by God, *because God reckoned him righteous, and he discovered it and believed it and so he reckoned himself righteous!*

...And thus, also, through faith Abel *received recognition from God!*

...He received confirmation to his faith! ...He received confirmation to that faith discovery! ...He received confirmation to that eternal truth he believed and embraced!

I say again: **God didn't recognize Abel's sacrifice; God recognized** *Abel's heart;* <u>**his faith,**</u>

...and He gave Abel approval, and recognition,

And thus, Abel received recognition from God *...and God reckoned him righteous!*

...because of his <u>*heart*</u>*!*

...Because it is <u>with the heart</u> one believes unto righteousness!

...And thus, God gave Abel approval and recognition.

God reckoned him righteous! *...because of his faith!*

The word *"RECKON"* has to do with **doing a sum** *and coming to it's ultimate accurate mathematical conclusion.*

Thus, the word *"RECKON"* can also mean **that an ultimate conclusion is reached, <u>and full recognition is mutually received and embraced</u>,** *because two parties are in total absolute agreement, and accurately so, because the math is correct!*

Isn't that just beautiful?!

Hallelujah!

Thank you for revealing these things to us God!

Chapter 9

Seeing As God Sees!

Notice what God said also to Abel's brother.

God said to Cain, in Genesis 4:7,

"If you do well, will you not be accepted?"

"And if you do not do well, Sin is crouching at the door; its desire is for you,"

"...but you must master over it!"

What does this *"do well"* refer to here?

It refers to the fact that we all must come **to the same accurate faith conclusion** Abel came to!

If we do, we will be able to *"master over"* sin.

But if we do not *"do well;"* if we **do not come to the same faith conclusion** Abel came to, we will not be able to *"master over"* sin, in fact, sin will *"master over"* us!

Can you see that, even in this scripture, it is clear that, **Sin is the *fruit of unbelief!***

...and it is also clear that **Sin is a living thing!**

Now how can sin just be a choice, when **Sin is a thing?** *...a living thing?*

Sin is a living thing!

Let's read Genesis 4:7 again. It says,

"If you do well, will you not be accepted?"

"And if you do not do well, Sin is crouching at the door; its desire is for you,"

"...but you must master over it!"

So, **Sin is a living thing.**

Sin has a *"desire!"*

Sin has a *life!*

It is alive! ...if you know what I mean,

I mean, Sin is death, **but it has a life,**

...just like sickness is death, *but has a life of its own;* **it has a life within it,** *a life-force* **at work within it, inside itself,**

...So, even though it has **its own life-force at work within it,** *sickness is something that is out of balance,*

...it is **another life force,** *other than your life-force, or God's life-force,* working inside you!

It is inside you, *just like Sin gets inside you.*

260

Sin is a life inside you, *working within you!*

...It's an outside force, *working within you,* against you!

...It is a negative life-force; *a death-force, working within you,* against you!

But hallelujah, we have been redeemed from that *life-force,* from that life of sickness and of sin!

...from those forces of death at work within us!

Genesis 4:7,

"...if you do not do well, Sin is crouching at the door"

"...its desire is for you,"

Do you see that?

"...its desire is for you,"

So, if something goes wrong within you ...if your heart isn't right ...if it is not well with your soul, with your being,

"...if you do not do well," (...if you are not well ...if it is not well with your being; if you are believing the wrong things),

"Sin is crouching at your door."

And so at the end of Genesis 4:7, God says,

*"...**but you must master over it!**"*

But how God, how do I do that?

He says, right there in the beginning of that same verse,

*"**If you do well, will you not be accepted?**"*

In other words, *"**If you do well,**"*

(If you align yourself with eternal truth and believe what you should believe, and embrace what is best for you, and live that out!)

*"...**you will be accepted!**"*

*...**meaning, if you do well,** (if you believe eternal truth, accurately, and you don't give into the lie, then) **you don't need to sneak around in life, and feel all terrified and concerned,***

*...**wondering when the next opportunity to sin is going to come,***

*'...**and I wonder if it is going to be bigger than the last time, and oh, I hope it's not too big for me, and stronger than me,***

*...**and maybe it's around this corner, or that corner, or the next corner.**'*

Hey, no, listen, righteousness does not think this way; *those who know they are righteous, who know their righteousness do not think this way!*

...**The righteous are full of faith, their righteousness is a fruit of faith, and therefore the righteous are as bold as a lion,** *just as confident, just as sure, just as full of assurance* ...*and no weapon formed against them shall prosper.*

"...if you do not do well, if it is not well with you, if it is not well with your soul, if it is not well with your faith, if you are not sure, and confident, full of the assurance of faith, full of truth and persuasion, and faith, full of conviction, concerning your righteousness, Sin is crouching at the door,"

...*it's just waiting there man, waiting to devour you!*

What door?

The door of doubt, confusion, and unbelief!

He is referring to that choice, that way of life which chooses to live life in isolation, in separation, *away from God!*

'I'm not doing so well as far as my faith is concerned man, as far as my convictions and assurance are concerned,'

'...so I'm just going to choose this thing, I'm just going to open this door and walk into this thing!'

'...this thing that is desiring me!'

'...this strong desire, and misplaced passion!'

...So with my own choice I walk into that door of doubt and unbelief and confusion, *and so now I find that Sin and its desire is there, waiting for me, and it is ready to leap and devour me!*

The word, *"crouching"* in the Hebrew, speaks of **a literal thing, a monster that is ready to leap, and grab you!**

"...but you must master it!"

"...you must master IT!"

"...you must master Sin!"

"...you must MASTER it!"

"...YOU must master it!"

...**Nobody else is going to master it for you, not even God!**

"...YOU MUST master it!"

I say again: *"...you MUST MASTER Sin!"*

That's exactly what God said to Cain!

And if God said it to him, *then it must have still been available, and possible,* to resist Sin, and overcome its fruit of sin, <u>*even after the Fall*</u>!

God was not hanging a proverbial carrot in front of Cain, you know, *teasing him with something he couldn't have!*

...teasing him with something that was, just out of reach!

Can you see here that **God does not recognize the Fall?!** ...God does not recognize *the dominion of Sin?!* ...And that God doesn't want Man *to recognize the dominion of Sin* either?!

Why?

Not just because Sin will devour us if we do, *but because <u>there is a greater reality about our lives</u>!*

Our design is still intact!

Our design is GREATER!

We can have righteousness, *by faith!*

We can enjoy every aspect of righteousness!

God wants to let Man know, *and He wants to say to Man,*

"Listen, I want you to dominate!"

"I want you to master it!"

"I want you to master over sin!"

…yet, from Adam to Moses, death reigned,

…But, thank God, <u>not over everyone</u>,

…but unfortunately over most!

And exactly why is that?

Because, even if they have a zeal, *it is not enlightened!*

They may even have a zeal for God, *but it is not enlightened!*

And that is the problem,

Romans 10:3, clearly tells us,

"For being ignorant of (righteousness, by faith,) …being ignorant of the righteousness that come form God, (and has been given to us as a gift, in the beginning, and has been ours all along, from the very beginning, and which can still be enjoyed through faith)"

(…being ignorant of that righteousness, that it was never taken away, that, even

though we lost it, it has always been ours, it has always been there, to access, by faith)

"For being ignorant of the righteousness that comes from God,"

"...being ignorant of that righteousness; the very righteousness of God;"

(God's righteousness; His image and likeness within us; and who He is as our Father, our Daddy ...being ignorant of His heart of love and acceptance towards us, and of the life we can enjoy in union and romance and oneness with Him, in the now)

"...For being ignorant of <u>that</u> righteousness, and seeking to establish their own (through all kinds of efforts of their own, all kinds of religious efforts and works), *therefore they did not submit to God's righteousness."*

I love what Paul says in verse 4, he says,

"For (indeed, or in spite of all that) *Christ is the end of the Law,"*

(...the end of any religious pursuits, no matter what kind they are,)

"For Christ is the end of the Law, so that every one who has faith may be justified,"

...may be made righteous!

The NKJV says,

"For Christ is the end of the Law for righteousness, to everyone who believes!"

...Christ spells the end of the use of the Law to try and pursue,

...to try and obtain, righteousness!

You cannot pursue righteousness *as if you have never had it!*

...And you cannot obtain *what you have always had!*

You can only be *awakened* to it!

Righteousness is now, *and always has been, <u>a faith issue</u>.*

What is faith?

Faith is *seeing* as God sees!

...seeing yourself as God sees you!

To have faith, is to see, and embrace, your righteousness!

To fully see, and embrace, your original true design, and your true identity in the Father, as His kids, His image and likeness, partakers of the Divine nature, *in spite of the Fall!*

...that is what righteousness, by faith, is all about!

...knowing, *and believing,* that intimate relationship, friendship and fellowship with God, is available to you, *right now!*

It is available, to everyone who believes it is!

It is available, *by faith!*

Acceptance, and approval, and recognition by God, are therefore also available, *by faith!*

...By seeing and believing the truth revealed!

God is pleased with such a faith!

...with a pursuit of Him, of fellowship with Him, based on such a faith!

It is that heart, and that faith, that pleases God!

Without that kind of heart, and that kind of faith,

...without knowing, *and believing,* the love God has for us, *it is impossible to please God!*

"...without faith, it is impossible to please God!"

"...to give God pleasure!"

Without knowing, *and believing,* the love God has for us, *without that kind of faith,* it is impossible *to enter in and enjoy your righteousness,*

...without that kind of heart, without knowing, *and believing,* the love God has for us, *without that kind of faith,* it is impossible *to enjoy righteousness with God,*

...enjoying intimate fellowship,

...and receiving approval and recognition because of it,

...because of faith,

...because of righteousness,

...receiving it and experiencing it on the basis of that faith and of that righteousness!

"...without faith, it is impossible to please God!"

"...to give God pleasure!"

...because every time you draw near, you will find yourself pulling away at the same time!

I say again: **Without faith being fully established in you,** *without the faith of God,*

...without knowing about yourself what God knows to be true about you all along,

...without seeing yourself the way God sees you,

...without seeing yourself that way; *as righteous and blameless, and welcome, and accepted,*

...without seeing these things clearly and believing them, *you will pull away every time you try to draw near!*

And why is that?

Because your own heart, *your own condemnation will keep you out!*

Why was Cain's sacrifice not received?

Because of his heart!

Because God could see right through him!

God could read Him like a book, and saw the corruption in his heart.

He could see the motives of his heart!

...and those motives weren't pure!

...they weren't purified through faith!

...like Abel's was!

God did not welcome and receive Cain's offering,

...because of the casual, flippant kind of attitude, in his pursuit of an inferior kind of relationship with God!

You see, he was willing to welcome some religion into his heart, a little bit of it, you know, just so he can at least be acknowledged by God, and that would have sufficed, that would have been a convenient scenario for him, a convenient relationship with God, whereby he could still keep God at arms length, you know, and only call on Him when he needed Him, *but he didn't really want to intimately know God and give God his whole heart!*

No wonder God rejected his sacrifice,

...because of the casual, flippant kind of attitude, in his pursuit of an inferior kind of relationship with God!

...because of the works mentality involved!

You see faith was not involved!

His sacrifice didn't have faith in it!

Oh, he worked and sacrificed alright, *but there was no faith behind any of it, or in any of it!*

Instead, it had religion written all over it; it had foolishness and presumption in it, *but not faith!*

All his works and his sacrificing *didn't have faith in it!*

Because there was no revelation there!

His pursuit was not the fruit of revelation!

He simply presented God with his own efforts, with the fruit of His own toil and hard labor, *to try and impress God and get His approval!*

...instead of pleasing Him!

Cain was only after that approval, you see,

...but nothing else, nothing real and substantial with God!

He did not truly pursue intimate fellowship with God!

God was not his life!

Friendship with God was not the motivating factor of his life!

He probably pursued recognition with God and made that sacrifice, *merely out of jealousy of, and competition with,* his brother Abel,

…mimicking everything Abel did, even bringing his own offering and sacrifice, and thinking he was going to get the same results!

But his heart wasn't pure!

God wasn't truly the passion and desire of his heart!

Cain was merely busy with religion!

Ignorance, a casual approach, no matter how sincere, is nothing but religion!

…a mockery of that which is sacred to God!

Religion is a mockery to God!

Cain just wanted approval *but he didn't really want righteousness!*

He just wanted approval *without righteousness!*

He just wanted recognition *without putting God first,*

He just wanted recognition *without pursuing intimacy and fellowship!*

…without pursuing righteousness by faith!

You can read it there in Genesis 4:4 & 5,

"...and Abel brought one of the firstlings of his flock and of its fat portions. And the Lord had regard for Abel and his offering,"

"...but for Cain and his offering He had no regard!"

*"**So Cain** (instead of being distraught and broken hearted, like his brother would have been if he was given the cold shoulder ...Cain, instead, being full of wrong unfulfilling pursuits, and rotten attitudes), **became very angry!**"*

Cain was doing exactly what his mom and dad did, *trying to cover their nakedness in their own efforts.*

Besides fruit, **leaves are also the fruit of trees.**

Cain also offered up leaves, *just like his parents did, to cover themselves up* ...to try and cover their nakedness before God.

Those leaves must have been from the tree of the knowledge of good and evil!

...I believe they were, amen!

*...Can you see with me that **besides the actual fruit of that tree, those leaves were also the fruit of that tree** ...the tree of works, of self-indulgence and hard work, and annoyances, and heartaches, and frustrations, and impurity and self-effort and curses!*

It is particularly compelling to notice that Adam and Eve tried to cover their nakedness, **but they failed, they couldn't properly cover themselves.**

God had to come and speak their inferior fallen language of punishment due, and sacrifices, and judgment handed out, *to provide them with an animal skin for clothing, and so to clothe them with yet another inferior covering, temporarily, in His presence, just to make them feel better about themselves.*

...But without greater revelation into eternal truth, *this was at best a temporary solution, only appropriate during a time of perceived offense and broken relationship!*

All this is of course a prophetic picture of using the Law as a covering, **yet another inferior covering** *as a replacement for what is real and authentic and original; our true righteousness, our true design.*

You see, that sacrifice, that temporary inferior covering, could give Adam and Eve some kind of standing before God, *similar to the standing under the Old Covenant,*

...because, in that sacrifice, in that death, there was no resurrection,

...only a death.

In that sacrifice there was a shedding of blood, and the indication of covenant, *therefore their conscience could be ministered unto,*

...but it could not be fully cleansed.

They still had to look forward in faith to the Seed, to the Messiah, who was going to come **and reveal to them,** *in His blood, in His death and resurrection,* **their true value and worth,** *based on His immense love for them*

...**revealing to them,** *their true eternal forgiveness, and innocence,* <u>based on their eternal righteousness</u>, **and thus cleanse them, totally, permanently!**

You see, as long as you see the blood of Jesus as yet another sin covering, yet another price paid for sin, *your conscience cannot be fully cleansed!*

Only once we fully recognize what Jesus actually came to accomplish, and what the blood of Jesus actually reveals, concerning the love of God for us, and concerning our eternal righteousness; our eternal value and worth, can our faith come alive, and our conscience finally be fully cleansed!

Only the blood of Jesus could do that fully, only the Godhead's undignified extreme demonstration of Their eternal love for us, based on our eternal value and worth, based on our eternal righteousness still intact, *could make our faith come alive!*

...That's why that little innocent animal sacrifice God made, **was only a prophetic picture of the One who was to come, of that Seed, Christ Jesus,** instead of being and providing a real covering, a long term, permanent solution, for Adam and Eve's nakedness!

...It was only a prophetic picture of the One who was to come, that ultimate Seed, Christ Jesus, *who would ultimately come and finally crush the head of the Serpent,* **and finally cleanse the conscience, once and for all, and open up the new and living way,**

...the original way restored,

...the way of faith.

But, I want us to see and know that righteousness by faith *was still available to them,* **even then, to a limited measure,** *until the fullness of time would come and all would be revealed in much greater detail.*

...so that faith could finally be based on substance, on real understanding, in depth understanding, instead of some vague mysteries.

You see, God instinctively knew that faith would need a stronger foundation, *so that the reign of righteousness could be complete and absolute!*

You see, in order for Sin to lose its mastery, in order for the reign of righteousness to be

fully established, upon a stronger foundation, *the original righteousness, the very faith of God, had to be revealed to the full; <u>it had to be re-revealed and understood to the full</u>!*

Hebrews 11:39 & 40 says,

"And all these, though well attested to by their faith, did not receive the fullness of what was promised,"

"Since God had foreseen the better things for our time, therefore, apart from us, they could not be totally made perfect!"

They, together with us, were only made complete when Jesus finally came, and actually died and was raised, *to reveal and make more sure and steadfast,* **that eternal righteousness** that they already somewhat enjoyed, and that we can now enjoy to the full, by faith; *in full assurance of faith!*

The Messiah did not come in their day, but in ours, and not actually even in ours, but actually well over 2000 years ago, *so we now can live in the absolute fullness and clarity of these things!*

1 Peter1:10-12 says,

"The prophets who prophesied, of the grace that was to be yours, searched and inquired about this salvation; ...They inquired what person or time was indicated by the Spirit

of Christ within them, when predicting the sufferings of Christ, and the subsequent glory!"

"It was revealed to them that they were serving, not themselves, but you, in the things which have now been announced to you, in the gospel, by those who preached (and still preaches) the gospel to you, through the Holy Spirit sent from Heaven,"

Through animal sacrifices under the Old Covenant, you could be restored to some kind of inferior religious fellowship with God, *but not really, not fully, not totally, not in complete intimacy and romance, <u>the kind that faith affords you</u>,* because you see, it was just a temporary covering, an inferior covering, it was nothing but an empty religious covering, *it wasn't real, it was just a shadow,* it was just a prophetic thing!

…a mere picture, *pointing to the real thing, the real substance of the thing,*

...*pointing to that real righteousness, that original righteousness* that would be restored in full, in the fullness of time, in Jesus.

...*Thus, the Old Testament animal sacrifices, the whole Old Covenant, the entire Jewish religion, as well as all the other religions of the entire human race, **and their inferior religious fake fellowship with God,*** was a mere picture, a prophetic picture, ***a mere shadow,*** pointing to the real thing, to the **real**
280

substance that would finally be revealed and restored in full, in Jesus!

Intimate relationship with God, relating to Him as Daddy and as a real companion in life, and for life, was very limited, decidedly limited before Jesus came!

…**but there was still some kind of recognition available there, even during the days of the Law, even under the Old Covenant times. (All you would need to do is to look at king David to see it).**

…**and it afforded them a fellowship with God,**

…*but not quite to the degree, to the fullness that we can enjoy the fullness of God's friendship and intimate fellowship today!*

…and so it was with Adam and Eve also,

…*there was still some kind of recognition towards Adam and Eve, there in that sacrifice of that young innocent animal,*

…*because God gave them clothing,*

…*but He still sent them out, out of that Garden.*

You see we need to get a clear grasp on this thing, *this reign of righteousness* that Adam and Eve lost,

...but that Abel was able to enter into, to some degree, through faith,

...and which has now been **fully restored *to us,***

...and is now being **fully restored *in us,*** through the Holy Spirit of Truth; the Spirit of wisdom and revelation *into the knowledge of Him,* **into the gospel.**

Our original righteousness is being fully restored to us, *through the gospel, and in the gospel!*

And so, I find it mighty interesting that God said, even to Cain, *about the reign of righteousness,* there in Genesis 4:7,

*"...**Sin is crouching at the door, but you must master over it!***"

That speaks of dominion!

...but, the problem with Cain was that, *death was in dominion,*

...and before the reign of righteousness can again become established,

...he had to first get *a revelation.*

...**And through that revelation, *his heart had to change* towards death, towards a life trapped in death, towards that death that was in him, *and he then also had to have a*** *desire quickened in him* for intimate fellowship with God, **through that revelation.**

…In other words he had to **desire righteousness.**

…**But, faith had to be birthed in his heart first.**

You see, for us as well,

…**before that reign of righteousness can again be established,**

…**the dominion of death, that separation from God and its consequences, has to be broken through faith.**

Faith breaks the dominion of death!

Faith ends the illusion of separation from God!

…**And thus, faith ends separation from God!**

Can you see that the reign of Sin has to be broken also, through faith!

…**So that the reign of righteousness and ongoing intimate fellowship with God, that romance, can be maintained!**

So, faith then also breaks the dominion of sin.

...**Faith; revelation knowledge, breaks the dominion of separation, and the dominion of death, the dominion of sin,** *and it establishes and strengthens the reign of righteousness!*

You see before the dominion of righteousness could again become established over the human race, *that law of sin and death, that dominion of death and sin, that separation between Man and God, that illusion of separation, had to be broken,*

...**God had to come in person,** *Jesus had to come* ...*that Law of Identification, through the incarnation, had to take affect,*

...*and Jesus had to die and be raised and elevated to heavenly places.*

He had to come and personally take upon Himself, that Law of Sin and Death, **and speak its inferior language;** *He had to speak our inferior language inherited from that other knowledge, the inferior knowledge of the tree of good and evil,* and thus, He had to take upon Himself ...*that punishment that was our due, (or that we were convinced was our due, through that poisonous fruit we swallowed, through the lies and deception we embraced,* **even though as far as God was concerned, we never really deserved.** As far as God was concerned, *we didn't deserve punishment;* as far as God was concerned, *we deserved mercy* more than judgment, and *we deserved revelation* more than punishment*)*

...God had to take that law of sin and death upon Himself,

...so that God could acknowledge Man again, *through that Law of Identification,*

...so that God could recognize and associate fully, there on the cross, with Man's death there in the garden,

...and Man's embrace of the punishment and the judgment and the torment of that hell,

...and thus, *through the Law of Identification,* God fully recognized and associated with Man's Fall, *even as far as going down into his hell with him,*

...He went down to hell with us, and we were in Him still, and therefore He also then *fully recognized Man,* through the Law of Identification, He fully associating with Man and recognizing *Man's resurrection from the dead,*

...*through the resurrection of Jesus from the dead,*

...*and through the resurrection of the dead*

...*in Jesus* (...even <u>that</u> was a prophetic symbol and a sign. - Matthew 27:52-53.)

285

…It all happened, so that God could recognize and acknowledge Man again,

…recognizing Man's position, *restored at His right hand*

…*through that Law of Identification.*

Thus, your belief in God doesn't define God; *His belief in you defines you!*

God's faith defines you! God's faith *in what He knows to be true about you* defines you!

You see, the right hand of God, speaks of the seat of authority!

…the place of authority!

So, God wants to restore us *in absolute authority!*

…in complete dominion, in Christ Jesus!

…*abiding,* in Christ Jesus!

…as we *abide* in Him, through faith, *He abides in us!*

…and thus, He in us, *restores our reign!*

Oh hallelujah!

Thank you Jesus!

Chapter 10

Out Of All Proportion!

Let's go back to Romans 5:15-21,

"The gift of God's grace, through the one man, Jesus, has far more powerfully affected mankind."

"God's act of grace, is out of all proportion, to Adam's wrong doing!"

Verse 16,

"And the free gift, is not like, the affect of that one Man's sin."

Praise God!

It is *out of all proportion* to the affect of that one Man's sin.

It is *out of all proportion* to <u>that</u> sin!

It is *out of all proportion* to Sin!

"For the judgment, following one trespass, brought condemnation,"

"...but the free gift (apart from the Law, and which has nothing to do with trespasses),

following (even after) many trespasses, brings righteousness!"

Verse 17,

The Albert Allen Conibear Translation says,

"For, if the reign of death was established, by the one Man, Adam,"

"...far more, shall the reign of life be established, in those, who receive the overflowing fullness of the free gift of righteousness by the one man, Jesus Christ!"

I want us to meditate in this, to muse on this, to think upon it, and ponder on it, and marinate in it, *so that that revelation* **will come _alive_ in us!**

The RSV says,

"If, because of one Man's trespass, death reigned, through that one Man, Adam"

*"...**much more, will those, who receive** (The Greek is in the past tense, thus)* ...**much more will those who _have received_ the abundance of grace and the free gift of righteousness** (included in that grace, _be able to_), **reign in life, through the one man, Jesus Christ!"**

Verse 18,

*"**Then,** (in conclusion), (just) **as one Man's trespass, led to condemnation for all men,**"*

*"**...so now, one man's act of righteousness, leads to righteousness and life for all men!**"*

My RSV translation says, *"**acquittal**"*

It says, *"**...so now, one man's act of righteousness, leads to acquittal and life for all men!**"*

Ha... ha... ha... Hallelujah!

That works for me too, amen!

...I just love that word, *"**acquittal,**"* but the actual Greek word used there, is the word, *'DIKAIOSIN'* which is the word for, **righteousness,** even though it is often translated as **justification** or **acquittal.**

*"**...so now, one man's act of righteousness, leads to righteousness and life for all men!**"*

Verse 19,

*"**For, by one Man's disobedience, many were made sinners,**"*

*"**So, by one man's obedience,** (the same) **many will be made righteous!**"*

Verse 20,

"The Law came in, to increase the trespass,"

The NKJV says,

"Moreover, the Law entered, that the offense may abound."

I have expounded on this in detail in my book *"Resurrection Life Now"* and *"God's Measure verses Man's Measure,"* but just to bring you up to speed quickly,

In Romans 7, Paul explains, how in ignorance, Sin is thought to lie dormant, *but the dominion of death was there all along,*

…and now then, the Law came in and said,

'You should not and must not!'

…**and suddenly now, Sin found opportunity by the Law, to stretch its muscles, and show its power,**

…**and, it thus even further established, and extended, its dominion,**

…**so that, Sin could be shown to be sin, and wrong for us, *beyond measure!***

"Moreover, the Law entered, that the offense may abound."

"But, where sin abounded, <u>grace abounded much more</u>!"

The RSV says,

"The Law came in, to increase the trespass."

"...but, where sin increased, <u>grace abounded all the more</u>!"

"...grace abounded all the more!"

Hallelujah!

"...grace abounded, much more!"

You see, *it abounded, much more!*

"...grace abounded, all the more"

Why?

Grace abounded, *because God wanted to restore, fully, the dominion of righteousness!*

For no other reason!

Grace did not abound, so we can continue in sin, and still pretend to be right with God!

No!

Grace abounded, *all the more,*

...much more!

...so that, righteousness can be <u>fully</u> restored!

God had the <u>full</u> restoration of righteousness in mind!

God wanted to restore, *the dominion of righteousness,*

...so grace had to <u>exceed</u> the dominion of Sin!

...grace had to <u>exceed</u> the affect of Sin!

If grace could not exceed the affect of Sin, the power of Sin, the way Sin affected us,

...then, not one man, other than Jesus, *could be made righteous!*

Grace had to <u>exceed</u> the affect of Sin!

And where did grace <u>exceed</u> the affect of Sin?

What was the affect of Sin?

Death!

Where did grace <u>exceed</u> the affect of Sin?

In the resurrection!

Through the resurrection!

Through the resurrection, the grace of God *exceeded*, the affect of Sin,

...the grace of God triumphed, *and it conquered Sin and Death.*

You see, victory had to be established, *on the basis of merit, or achievement; greater merit!*

What Jesus did; *what He revealed and demonstrated, <u>out-achieved</u>* the Devil and the Sin that came into the world through him and which was introduced to the rest of us, through Adam.

...because what Jesus did had greater merit!

If we had a dart competition going on, and I get 50 points, but you get 60 points, *then who's achievement is going to win!*

Who is going to be declared the winner?

You are!

Why?

Because you <u>exceeded</u> my capabilities, *and my performance; my abilities!*

Can you see that Jesus' performance, through His resurrection, <u>exceeded</u> *the performance of death!*

It *exceeded* the result of Adam's sin!

It *exceeded* the power of Sin!

It *exceeded* the power of the Law of Sin and Death!

Romans 4:25 says that,

"He (Jesus), was put to death, on account of our trespasses, or, because of our trespasses, or by our trespasses,"

"...and, He was raised, on account of, or because of, our righteousness!"

...on the account of us officially being declared innocent, and therefore restored to righteousness again!

...on account of Sin's power, being broken; and that death, being broken,

...and death itself, living life in separation from God, being broken!

...and so, because of that, we can now enjoy righteousness,

...we can enjoy the dominion and the reign of righteousness again!

Through His resurrection, *Jesus raised us up, to newness of life!*

Can you understand the abundance of grace now?

I have another book written about this, called, *"Grace Exceedingly Sufficient,"* and you might want to get that one and read it as well.

Can you understand *the measure* in which grace abounded?

In what *measure* did grace abound?

It abounded, in *the fact that grace <u>exceeded</u>, the affect of Adam's sin, and Satan's Sin ...which was death!*

Through the introduction of Sin, death came into the equation, amen.

...Thus, through Sin *came death*.

Romans 5:12,

"*Sin, entered the world, through one Man, Adam, and death, through Sin.*"

When grace *exceeded* the affect of Sin,

...*when grace exceeded death, and death was dealt with, and its dominion broken,*

...*then, the dominion of Sin was broken.*

The dominion of Sin was broken, you see!

Now, I want you to see where the dominion of righteousness comes in!

The dominion, or the reign of righteousness, is established legally and vitally, *in actuality, and in all reality,*

...through the reign of Jesus Christ!

...through the reign, of the life, of Jesus Christ!

In other words: *Through the resurrection!*

...through the continual reign of the resurrection,

...through the resurrection life of Jesus Christ!

...through that resurrection power of God!

...that eternal life; that Zoe of God!

The reign of righteousness, is established, *on the fact, that the power and dominion of death, is broken.*

That death, **which separated us from righteousness, and from God, is broken!**

Grace abounded, you see!

Grace abounded, *all the more!*

There is <u>much more power</u> in grace!

Under grace,

...under the influence of that grace,

...under the influence, of the truth of the gospel,

*...***you are set free!**

296

Under the influence of that faith,

...under grace,

...Sin shall not be your master,

...but you master over it!

Oh, Hallelujah!

"...grace abounded, <u>all the more</u>,"

Verse 21,

"...so that, <u>just as</u>, Sin reigned, through death,"

"...so now, <u>just so</u>, grace now, might reign, through righteousness!"

"...to eternal life, through Jesus Christ, our Lord!"

I especially love the way this whole passage is translated in the Mirror Study Bible. Let's start reading there from verse 11, and we'll end here again, in verse 21:

5:11 Thus, our joyful boasting in God continues; Jesus Christ has made reconciliation a reality.

5:12 One person opened the door to [1]**sin. Sin introduced** *(spiritual)* **death. Both sin and death had a global impact. No one escaped its tyranny.**

The footnote there is very interesting. It reads:

*(The word translated, "**sin**" is the word
₁HAMARTIA, from HA, **negative,** and MEROS,
portion or **form, thus to be without your
allotted portion,** or **without form,** pointing to
a disoriented, distorted identity; the word,
MEROS is the stem of, MORPHE, as in 2
Corinthians 3:18. The word, METAMORPHE,
with form, is thus the exact opposite of,
HAMARTIA, **without form.** Thus, the word
"sin" is **to live out of context with the
blueprint of one's design; to behave out of
tune with God's original harmony.**)*

**5:13 The law did not introduce sin; it was
just not pointed out yet.**

**5:14 In the mean time death dominated
everyone's lifestyle, from Adam all the way
till Moses,** *(2500 years before the law was
given),* **no one was excluded; even those
whose sins were different from Adam's.**
*(well, almost no one; the exceptions are
miniscule.)* **The point is and the fact is that
Adam's ₁deviation set sin into motion – but
what happened to mankind because of one
Man, Adam, is in principle typical of what
was about to happen to the same mankind
because of the one man, Jesus!**

The footnote says:

*(Paul now employs a word which only he
uses in his epistles, PARABASIS, instead of
the usual word for "**sin**," HAMARTIA.*

PARABASIS *has two components,* PARA, *which points to **a close proximity,** as in **union,** and* BAINOS, **step, footstep** – *in this sense,* **a deviation,** *thus;* **out of step – out of sync.** *In Adam mankind became* **out of sync** *with their true identity, but didn't know it until the law revealed it. In Christ the same mankind **was revealed to be, and thus became, exceedingly righteous** but do not realize it until the gospel reveals it.)*

5:15 The only similarity in the comparison between the ₁crash-landing and the gift, is that both Adam and Christ represent the masses. However, the grace gift lavished upon mankind in the one man, Jesus Christ, supersedes the effect of Adam's failure, by far, and is thus beyond comparison in significance to the idea of ₂death and separation.

The footnote again:

(Now Paul introduces the word, ₁PARAPTOMA, *from* PARA, **closest possible proximity,** *as in* **union,** *and* PIPTO, **to descend from a higher place to a lower – to stop flying.** *No wonder he urges us in Colossians 3:1-3 to **engage our thoughts with the things that are superior, or above, where we are now co-elevated to and jointly enthroned in, in the heavenlies, together with Christ!** The word,* ₂APOTHNESKO, **death,** *suggests* **a separation;** *from* APO, *meaning* **any kind of separation of one thing**

from another, by which the union or close fellowship of two is destroyed; also speaking of *a state of separation and distance.* The word, THNESKO means death.

"But, God's free gift immeasurably outweighs the transgression. For if, through the transgression of the one individual, Adam, the mass of mankind have died, infinitely greater is the generosity wherewith God's grace, and the gift given in His grace, which found expression in the one man, Jesus Christ, have been bestowed on the mass of mankind." - Weymouth Translation, 1912.)

5:16 The principle of the gift speaks a different language, and brings a radically different equation to the table. Whereas a single sin resulted in a judgment that concluded in condemnation; grace transcends it all, and therefore translates countless deviations into acquittal and innocence; declaring righteousness.

5:17 Thus, death no longer has the final say. Instead, life rules! If the effect of one Man's crash-landing engaged the whole of mankind in a death-dominated lifestyle, how much more advantaged is the very same mankind now that they are [1]the recipients of the [2]boundless reservoirs of grace, empowering them to enjoy the dominion of life through the gift of righteousness restored, because of that one man, Jesus Christ. Grace is 2out of all proportion in superiority to the transgression.

The footnote says:

*(No, grace is not something you qualify for by receiving it! Grace and its gift of righteousness restored **already belongs to mankind without their permission!** The words, 1OI LAMBANONTES do not mean, to believingly accept, but simply: **the recipients!** [It is written in the Present Active Participle Nominative tense.] The word, 2PERISSEIA means **super abundantly; that which exceeds all boundaries.** Of course it doesn't take faith out of the equation! **No, it gives context to faith, and amplifies it!** See verse 1 & 2. **Faith is not what you do, in order to; it's what happens to you, because of!**)*

5:18 The conclusion is clear: If one offense condemns the entire human race; then in principle, the righteousness of one vindicates the entire human race.

5:19 The disobedience of the one 1exhibits mankind as sinners; the obedience of another exhibits the same mankind as righteous instead.

*(The word, 1KATHISTEMI means, **to cause to be, to set up, to exhibit** – it can thus also closely relate to **a mirror image or reflection.** We were not made sinners however, by our*

301

*own disobedience; neither were we **revealed to be and therefore made righteous** by our own obedience.)*

5:20 The presence of the law made no difference, instead it merely highlighted the offense; but where sin increased, grace superseded it and overrides it.

5:21 Death provided sin its platform and power to reign from; now grace has taken over sovereignty through righteousness exhibited, *to re-introduce unthreatened life* under the preeminence (or ultimate superiority) of Jesus Christ, in His Lordship over us.

You see, God's grace was not revealed, *so that Man could just have an overdraft facility.*

…so that, Man could now just continue in sin,

…and God would still say,

'All right man, you know, I'm such a loving God, I'll just excuse you again for yet another time, and I'll leave you alone until another time,

I won't do anything about it, you know, maybe next time you'll get it right and won't do this anymore!

So don't worry about it, I've got you covered!'

See, that was life under the Law.

Israel sinned, and transgressed, *and the curse set in, and it pounded them into the ground, and into dust,*

...and then they cried out, and they *"repented"* or felt sorry for what they did, and said,

'Oh God, please have mercy!'

And then God would have mercy on them again, and God would feel sorry for them again, *and God in His grace gives them another chance!*

But now, you see, the grace of the Old Covenant was a different grace, *than the grace of the New Covenant!*

...And, unfortunately, it is exactly because people are still trying to live under the grace of the Old Covenant, rather than the New Covenant, that people still see God's grace as an overdraft facility!

Many believers, or should I say, religious people, a part of the so called "Church" system, have never actually received the <u>full knowledge</u> *of the New Covenant!*

Many have never quite received or believed the knowledge that <u>*we can conquer!*</u>

The man-made "Church-system, or structure," and their blind religious

followers, for the most part, *remains defeated, with a sin-consciousness!*

…and most of them think,

'Oh well, here I go again, I am such a weakling, and I'll just have to "repent" and cry, and feel sorry for myself again, and try and do better next time,'

…but then they just do it again, and they'll have to do the whole "repentance" thing all over again!

But listen, God wants to establish, the reign of Righteousness, *through faith,*

…through a thorough understanding of truth,

…through enlightened revelation into the New Covenant!

It is interesting to note that the word, *"repentance"* often used in our English Translations, comes from the English word, PENANCE (taken from the Latin, not the Greek), and it means, **to owe a fine, and therefore to have to make payment for that debt.** And then later the RE was added to the word PENANCE **to reveal that this would have to be a constant ongoing thing, (just like Old Testament sacrifices), and thus, the RE was added to PENANCE just *to get more guilt-mileage out of it,*** which in turn helped the clergy to more easily **manipulate**

and control their followers to built many expensive cathedrals and which also afforded the clergy **to be able to more easily milk the people in order to gain for themselves much personal comfort and luxury.**

The Greek on the other hand never uses the term *"repent"* or *"repentance,"* but instead it uses the word, METANOIA which comes from META, **together with,** and NOIS or NOIA, which means **thinking** or **mind** and refers to **one's thought process, or belief-system.**

Thus, MEATANOIA has to do with **God stepping in and helping us get on the same page as Him, renewing or transforming our thinking, our minds, our thought-process or mind-sets and belief-system, to line up more accurately with His.**

It is closely related to the word, METAMORPHO or METAMORPHOSIS, **transformation.**

And thus METANOIA **is something that happens to you, rather than merely something you do in your own will-power, by choice.**

You see, **greater truth has to be introduced in order to transform you belief-system and thinking-process;** you cannot simply change what you think or believe *with your heart*, it's not that simple, you can't just throw it out, at will. **As a person really thinks or believes deep in his heart, so is he.** - Proverbs 23:7.

Thus it takes revelation knowledge, it takes God, it takes the Holy Spirit engaging us through the word of truth, it takes METANOIA to transform our belief-system and thought-process or mind-set.

It is something that happens to us, through the gospel, through the truth of the Gospel revealed to us, rather than something we do by sheer will-power.

...Through revelation into New Testament truth, through that insight into the New Covenant, *through that faith,* God wants to put you into a position, to where, the abundance of grace, *can have it's full affect, in your life,*

...and it results in the reign of righteousness!

We need to see clearly, how the deception that the enemy operates in now, how it works!

We need to then also see, how the legal power of Sin is broken, *how the dominion of Sin is broken!*

But let's face it, Satan still operates powerfully over Man, even today still,

...he still operates with quite a measure of success!

...through Sin!

306

…and He could even trap Christians into sinning.

You see the moment deception sets in, *then the law of Sin sets in again,*

…and the power of Sin becomes affective again.

You need to see it, and keep that in mind, in your own life, and your own experience.

You see, when you as a believer sin, *you actually sin,* you know what I mean, *I mean that* **Sin, genuinely, immediately, gets a hold of you,**

…but now 1 John 2:1 & 2 says,

"My little children, I write this to you, so that you may not sin,"

*"…**but, *if* any one of you does sin, we have an advocate…**"*

Actually the Greek uses the word, PARACLETOS *rather than "advocate"*

You see, if the Law of Sin did not set in, *if it was just a choice,* **then we needn't have had a PARACLETE.**

A PARACLETE is one who comes to comfort, edify, exhort and strengthen. Both Jesus and the Holy Spirit comes along side us and use the truth, insight and revelation

into the truth, to persuade and convince us, more convincingly concerning who we are from God's perspective; from His point of view, from His vantage point. Thus a PARACLETE is there, the Holy Spirit of Truth is there, to use the ultimate truth, the legal grounds of it, the legitimacy of God's truth, to deal with legal matters.

Thus, you need a PARACLETOS when legal matters are involved.

And listen now; he is speaking to Christians now, here in 1 John 1 and 2.

And so, if a Christian sins, *he needs a PARACLETOS who knows legal matters, who knows the full legal ground, the legitimacy of God's truth, the absolute authority of it, in and out.*

You see, that Christian needs to be able to, by faith, appropriate fully Jesus Christ's expiation, on his behalf.

...and through that expiation Jesus accomplished,

...through that intervention of Jesus, backing up with resurrection power, that work of redemption,

...you can be released again, form that law of sin and death!

Hey, there is a big difference between the word, *"expiation"* and the word, *"propitiation"* used in error as its replacement in many of our English Translations.

John said in 1 John 2:2 of Jesus that ***"He Himself is the expiation for our sin, and not just for ours, but also for that of the whole world."***

John did not says, ***"He Himself is the <u>propitiation</u> for our sin"***

No, he said, ***"Jesus Himself is the <u>expiation</u> for our sin, and not just for ours, but also for the sin of the whole world."***

A simple meaning of the word, *"propitiation"* often used in our English Translations is **the act of appeasing, or making well-disposed a deity, thus incurring divine favor or avoiding divine retribution**.

...And then they add that *it is the action taken on our behalf by our intercessor, Jesus, standing in for us, and doing something on our behalf,* **in order to keep Divine retribution from coming upon us, or in order for us to be able to avoid Divine retribution.**

The word, "**propitiation**" has to do with the object of wrath, and it has to do with God being appeased, meaning that Jesus needed to try and assuage God's wrath by giving Him something that will satisfy Him and calm Him down, so that He won't come and mow us all down. So, if you are angry or you are violated, and I satisfy your anger, or appease you, then I am restored to your favor and the problem is either averted or removed altogether. And that my friends is what the word, "**propitiation**" is all about.

The prefix, **pro** means "**for**," so, "**propitiation**" supposedly now brings about the change in God's attitude, so that He moves from being at enmity with us, to being **for** us. Thus they say, through the process of "**propitiation**" we are being restored into fellowship and favor with God. It supposedly can be seen as part of a process; as God's ongoing process and effort in trying to change us and remake us in order to eventually present us as new creations.

The problem with all that is that this word, "propitiation" and its meaning, has no place in the New Testament Scriptures and is in direct conflict with the truth of the Gospel; *it's in itself a violation of the gospel and does not belong in any of our translations!*

The difference between "**expiation**" and "**propitiation**" is huge.

"**Propitiation**" has to do with a ransom that is supposedly owed, and now gets paid, whereas the word, "**expiation**" rather refers to God's heart, or the attitude of the One who supposedly have to be paid this ransom.

Do you see the difference?

In the word, "**expiation**" it is the prefix **ex** that is being emphasized and it means "**out of**" or "**from**," so "**expiation**" has more to do with the **source** of an action, rather than the action itself; or the **object** the action is focused upon.

Thus, the action that originates out of the source has to do with **the removing or taking away of something** actually unrelated to the source.

So, translate that into biblical terms and it means that **the action taken from God's heart, because of His goodness** has to do with **removing or taking away guilt permanently** *from us,* not from God, *thus bringing about atonement or at-one-ment in our hearts, better known as reconciliation.*

You see, **God was not in Christ, reconciling Himself to the world,** *appeasing Himself,* **but reconciling** *a wayward world* **to Himself;** *appeasing a deceived, misguided, confused and angry world.*

Big difference!

You see, it is beneath the dignity of God to supposedly have His wrath placated; *it is a total contradiction to His immense love for us* **that we should have to do something to supposedly soothe Him or appease Him.**

...As if He has an ego problem, or an anger management problem!

You are welcome to get my book, *"You are totally forgiven!"* *if you want to have a better understand of the Greek word, ORGE which often has been wrongly translated as, "**wrath**" in our English Translations, when it in fact means,* **passion** *and speaks of* **an expression of emotion, based on a strong desire or passion of the heart.** In that book I go into detail about several scriptures translated with the word, "**wrath**" in it, and show you how they *should be better translated to bring out the deeper insight and revelation God wanted to convey* **to our hearts, directly from His heart,** *in Paul's use of that Greek word, ORGE.*

You see, we need to thoroughly understand the incarnation and work of redemption, *and what God actually has to say to us in it,*

...and we also need to study, and comprehend the present day ministry of Jesus, *as it relates to what was revealed and accomplished in Him concerning us!*

If you do, you will soon discover that His intervention in your life and in my life, right now,

...is based on that expiation that was done, on our behalf, in that work of redemption,

...once and for all, for all men.

Sometimes we think Jesus' ministry ended well over 2000 years ago now,

312

…but no, **He is in ministry right now!**

Jesus is in a ministry office right now!

He has always been, and now is, and forever will be, our PARACLETOS!

He, as our eternal representative, is seated at and in and as the right hand of the Father forever,

…seated there as our intervener,

…as our PARACLETE,

…as a law enforcement agent,

…as an eternal testimony to God's eternal association and identification with us; God's approval and recognition of us; God's ultimate knowledge of us; God's ultimate truth!

*…***and His ministry is called,** *the ministry of reconciliation.*

That's why, our intercession for others in prayer right now, and our intervention in their lives, and our interaction with them, *is merely an extension of His ministry,*

…it is based on **what He has done,** and it cannot actually add anything to what He has done, *…but it is such a vital part of Jesus' ministry right now, in working together with Him* *now, to open people's eyes, **to the reality** of what **He has revealed** in what He did;*

…it's an active extension of His ministry right now.

Paul says,

*"**We, therefore, plead with you, we strongly make our appeal, we strongly appeal to you, <u>through the gospel</u>, proclaiming it on behalf of Jesus Christ, and our message is simple: <u>be</u> ye reconciled to God!**"*

…Thus, in our ministry we intercept, the attacks and the lies and the deception of the Devil; **through the truth of the gospel** we address and tear down Satan's stronghold in people's hearts and minds, *and we rescue them from that hell they have been living in because of it!*

…and so, we stand between him and his prey, *the human race,*

…and we come against him, not by directly trying to take him on, in some sort of supposed spiritual warfare prayer,

…and don't get me wrong now, okay; *if we have to cast devils out, we will, amen,*

...so I am not excluding that, …but we come against his attacks, and his plans, *by **introducing truth to the human race,***

314

...by preaching and teaching the true gospel,

...and we rescue their minds and their lives, from the snares of the Devil.

Let's go back to Romans 5 there, and let's go back to the RSV translation, and I want to actually get into Chapter Six now,

...but let's quickly go back to **Paul's conclusion** there in Romans 5:18-21,

*"Then, (in conclusion), **as one Man's trespass, led to condemnation for all men**,"*

*"...**so now, one man's act of righteousness, leads to righteousness and life for all men**!"*

*"For, by one Man's disobedience, **many were made sinners**,"*

*"So, by one man's obedience, **many will be made righteous**!"*

"The Law came in, to increase the trespass."

*"But where sin increased, **grace abounded all the more**!"*

*"...so that, **just as,** Sin reigned, through death,"*

*"...so now, **just so,** grace now, might reign, through righteousness!"*

"...resulting in (the enjoyment and living of) eternal life (The Godhead's own quality of life and love They enjoy in their fellowship circle of other-centered love),"

"...through Jesus Christ, our Lord!"

As I have said before, *God wants to establish, the reign of Righteousness, <u>through faith</u>,*

God wants to put you into a position, to where *the abundance of grace, can have its <u>full</u> affect, <u>in your life</u>,*

...resulting in the reign of righteousness!

Okay now, Romans 6:1,

"What shall we say then? Are we to continue in sin, that grace may abound?"

"Shall we just continue in sin, hoping that grace shall just continue to abound, in spite of our sin?"

"By no means!"

Another translation says,

"Not at all!"

In other words,

"Don't you dare think like that! Man, don't you even think like that!"

316

Another translation says,

"God forbid!"

Can you see how under religion people *have twisted the truth of the Scriptures?*

…because this is exactly what religion teaches!

The man-made Christian religion, in fact, all religion, teaches **absolutely contrary** *to what God, through Paul, was saying in Romans 6.*

Religion says,

'Oh well, we can just kind of, you know… I mean sin is just a normal thing, a normal part of life, a normal part of your Christian walk, and there has been provision made for that, you know,

…because God knows how we are, I mean, He knows about the Fall, and He knows how weak and inferior we are, and He knows we don't stand a chance against the Devil or the power of Sin, I mean, not really, we don't really stand a chance at beating the Devil, I mean he is so strong, and he has been at this a lot longer than we have, and so, you know,

…we can just kind of, try to ignore our sinfulness, as best we can, because we are just sinners saved by grace,

…thank God for grace, but we are just sinners, and we still have that old flesh and that old sin-

*nature inside us to deal with, and so, **we all sin brother, even the preacher sins**,'*

'…so sin is just the normal thing, just a normal part of Christian life!

…It's just the normal thing man, don't beat yourself up over it too badly now, because that will just lead to more unnecessary condemnation you know, and that's not what God had in mind,

*…so you just have to deal with it as best you can, so you can be happy, and you just have to kind of, you know, **accept the fact that sin is just a normal thing**'*

No, hey listen, *sin is not the normal thing!*

Oh may we stop thinking that way! **"God forbid" us thinking that way!**

What part of, *"God forbid,"* do you not understand?

"Are we to continue in sin, that grace may abound?"

"Not at all!"

"By no means!"

"God forbid" us thinking that way!

And why is that? …**Because something of much greater significance, of much greater**

318

truth, of much greater reality was revealed to us in Jesus Christ!

...and Jesus restored it to us!

...And so now here comes **the law of identification through faith,** and it comes into play again, **and it challenges us,**

Verse 2, the second part there,

"How can we who died to Sin, still live in it?"

In other words,

...How can we still live *in its fruit?*

...How can we still live in our sins, **which are the fruit of Sin?**

In other words,

...if we died to Sin, to that inferior identity, *how can we still live in it, how can we still live in its sins?*

Do you see how, legally, Man was identified with Adam's transgression?

Now you could argue, and go to court, and say,

'But I wasn't in the Garden; **I wasn't even there!'**

…and you can try and prove, that you weren't there, in the Garden,

…but vitally, in all reality, the implication of that transgression took you in its victory, and brought you under its control as well!

And so, legally, because of that law of identification, *you were made sin; it was imputed and imparted to you.*

…and thus you became a sinner.

But now, in the same argument,

…you could say that,

'But I was not on that cross; I wasn't there, I was not even alive, when Jesus died!'

…but legally, vitally, in all reality, by that same law of identification, **the implications of Jesus' victory took you into His triumph, and into His reign, and brought you under the repercussions and therefore also under the influence, and the power of grace!**

He brought you into the power of the law of the Spirit of life!

….and you see, the law of identification through faith, links you to that law of life, and to the reign of righteousness!

…It directly applies to you!

...and thus His resurrection life and power directly applies to you and is yours!

You see, in the sight of God, according to the faith of God, as far as God is concerned, *we all died,* there, in Jesus!

That's the faith of God!

That's what God believed, happened on that cross!

That's what God saw, when Jesus died!

That's what God sees, in the death of His Son!

He sees, the death of the whole human race!

He sees us all liberated *there, in the death of Jesus!*

He sees, the power of Sin broken, *and He sees us, free, from Sin's power, and its hold on us!*

That's what God knows, legally and vitally, and in all reality!

That's what God knows, happened on that cross and in that death and in that resurrection!

That's what God *knows* to be true!

That's what God *recognizes* to be the truth!

In the sight of God, that is exactly what happened!

We were crucified with Christ, in the sight of God!

...*in the sight of God!*

You see, that's what counts!

What law recognizes is what counts!

What the One who made all law, (all the laws of the universe), *what He recognizes, is what counts!*

ha... ha... ha... Hallelujah!

The highest seat of government, *God's own government,* recognizes the death of Jesus Christ, *as your death!*

God saw *you* hanging on that cross!

When Jesus was buried, *God saw you buried!*

God says,

'You're buried!'

Ha... ha... ha...

He saw *you* go down into hell!

...And so He said to Sin,

...He said to that marriage between us and Sin,

'Listen, you go down into Hell, where you belong!'

He saw the torment in Jesus' face, *and He saw your torment!*

...He saw you in torment!

He saw <u>you</u> receiving the full blow of the punishment Satan attached to you and said was your due!

...And He came to rescue you from it!

He saw the full blow of the curse *upon <u>us</u>,* when Jesus became as Sin *...when He literally, legally became, that Sin, and took it upon Himself, and took it away!*

...in the meantime the Devil poured all his hatred out on Jesus, and gave Him, the full blow of torment, and of the curse, and of death!

...and Jesus cried out, because of the full impact of the Law of Identification, He prophetically cried out, and partook of and echoed the cry of lost humanity,

"My God, My God, why have you forsaken Me!"

He was crying *our cry*!

And in the eyes of God, He saw all those things *done* to *you*,

He saw all that happened there, *as if it was happening to you*,

...and He couldn't hardly bear looking at such a sight any longer, because everything within Him wanted to set us free from it, with all His might!

And so, when Jesus died, *God the Father saw you die there!*

...and thus He saw the original you, the one who was made in is His image and likeness, fully restored and free there!

...because whatever happened to Jesus, in the eyes of God, in the mind of God, by the faith and knowledge of God, it literally, legally, vitally, in all reality, happened to us!

...And so, practically now, in our very own experience, as we embrace the very faith of God as our own, we enter into that victory of Jesus,

We enter into our freedom from Sin and Satan!

How?

Through that law of identification; *through that law of faith!* ...Through entering into that law of identification with Jesus,

...Through identifying with Jesus, *by faith*

...by embracing the very faith of God!

You see, we literally enter into the experience of that reality, *by faith!*

...by embracing the faith of God as our own,

...seeing what God saw!

...believing what God believes!

...knowing what God knows to be reality!

...embracing it ourselves fully, as <u>reality</u>!

And then, the same Spirit now, that raised Jesus from the dead, comes and confirms God's faith within you, within your heart, and He comes, and He dwells within you, right there in your mortal body,

...and He quickens you!

Listen, you truly are identified with Jesus, in His death!

Now He goes on to say here, through Paul, in Romans 6:2,

"How can we, who died to Sin, and its sin, still live in it?"

You see, in order for that law of identification to become vital,

…to become, a practical reality,

…a practical power, in our lives,

…*you must be in <u>faith</u>,*

…*you must embrace the faith of God, <u>fully</u>.*

…*you must be, fully persuaded,*

…*you must be, in total agreement!*

Let's take a look at verse 11,

"So, you also, must consider…"

…and the Greek word used there, is the word for, *"reckon."*

It means: ***to come to a correct mathematical conclusion*** **…to do the sum correctly, and come to a logical conclusion;** *a legal conclusion, an accurate conclusion.*

In other words, **you must come to an accurate conclusion in the truth, a practically viable conclusion;** *a vitally accurate conclusion, according to the laws of mathematics and of truth!*

It means: **you cannot** *afford* **to come to the** *wrong conclusion when it comes to math or truth for that matter,* **because it has practical binding affects;** *it has some very real consequences in this life!*

Verse 11,

"So, you also, must consider…"

"…you also, must <u>reckon</u>*, yourselves, dead to Sin, to that identity inherited in the Fall, and therefore dead to sins."*

"…you must <u>reckon</u> *yourselves, alive to God, in Christ Jesus!"*

Do you see how crucial it is, that we be renewed, in the Spirit; *in the spirit of our mind?*

You see, you can call yourself a Christian *…and you* <u>ARE legally free</u> *in Christ Jesus, amen,*

…but you can still live, practically, under that dominion of darkness!

Why?

Because you fail to <u>reckon</u> **yourself, dead to Sin!**

…you fail to <u>conclude</u> *yourself, dead to Sin!*

...you fail to <u>reckon</u> yourself, dead to your sins!

If a Christian still sins, *this is exactly their problem:* They fail to <u>reckon</u> themselves dead to sin,

...because they still live, under the dominion of a deceived mind!

The law of identification, as far as God is concerned, is only released, *the moment you come into total agreement with God, and actually believe!*

You see, God already <u>reckons</u> you alive in Christ Jesus!

But, if your mind is still operating in those old thinking patterns,

...then you still see yourself, guilty,

...you still see yourself, subject to sin.

And you see, while your faith is inaccurate and incomplete, while your mind is still accommodating sin, *then you are going to have to argue with the teachings of grace,*

...then you're going to have to argue against grace!

*...*and then you are going to argue about grace, *in the same weak way* these guys argued in verse 1 of Romans 6.

'Well we're just going to continue to sin, because God's grace abounds in any case'

No, that's not what the grace of God is there for, you silly goose you!

Ha... ha... ha...

The grace of God is there, *to release the gift of righteousness to you,*

...so that righteousness can then, *come into its reign, in your life!*

...*so that righteousness, so that your true identity as child of God,* (and not child of Joe and Susan so and so) ...*so that that righteousness, and true identity can come into total dominion, in your life,*

...*so that you would not let sin reign over you anymore!* ...*because you <u>reckon</u> yourself, included in that law of identification,*

In the faith of God, in the law of identification, <u>in that faith</u>, in that <u>same faith</u>, in the very faith of Jesus,

*'...**God reckons me, so now, <u>I reckon myself also</u>!***'*

...and there you go, of you go, and you live your life, *and it works!*

'I reckon myself, dead unto sin, but, alive unto God!'

God's intention with His grace, is to bring you back into a position of authority, *where you actually walk in authority, above sin.*

Now, 1 John 2:1 comes in, where John says,

"My little children, I write this to you, so that you may not sin!"

"…but if you do sin…"

IF you sin, not when you sin, but IF you do sin,

…God's not just going to wipe you out,

*…no, He has already provided you with a PARACLETOS, **Jesus the righteous; the one who fully represents our righteousness, and we are not just left in the dark and at a loss of what to do now, no, we do have a PARACLETOS, and so we remind ourselves of what He came and revealed and demonstrated!***

John says,

"But IF you do sin, we already have a PARACLETOS who is one with the Father, Jesus Christ the righteous."

So God's not just going to wipe you out, no, He is going to remind us of the ultimate

truth concerning us through the PARACLETOS, through the Holy Spirit of truth, who comes to remind us of the truth, because do *we have another PARACLETOS already, Jesus Christ!*

You see, the entire Godhead, Father Son, and Spirit are in total agreement, *and together they are all reminding us of the truth and straightening our thinking out through the truth, and stirring us up through the truth,* not to put up with the Devil, or with Sin, with that inferior identity, in our lives any longer.

Jesus did not and does not have to persuade the Father about us, no, *He came to persuade us about the Father.*

There is nothing in the incarnate Word, Jesus, that is *in conflict with who God the Father is!* - John 1:1-3.

Jesus said, *"If you underestimate Me, you underestimate My Father – and you underestimate you too!"* - John 14:11 (Mirror Study Bible).

...So, if Jesus then really is our PARACLETE, and the entire Godhead is in absolute agreement with what was revealed about us and restored to us in Him, then don't you then dare go and get yourself into a pit of despair, and guilt, condemning yourself, and thinking and believing and saying to yourself,

'Oh, I am just a useless old sinner!'

No man, **nonsense!**

Notice what it says over there in Romans 5:10,

"For, since while we were enemies, we were reconciled to God, by the death of His Son, <u>much more</u>, now that we are reconciled, shall we be saved, by His life!"

…and what is His life now?

It's His life in us, amen,

…but it's also His life, **His ministry at the right hand of the Father,** *amen!*

What is His life now?

His life now, His ministry now, **is the result of His resurrection.**

Paul says there in Romans 5:10,

"…much more,"

So if we had a chance then, while we were still sinners, *we've got a much better chance now!*

…and that is not to give us an excuse to sin, God forbid!

…but should you fall into sin, should you be snared into sin, and get tripped up by sin, and get tangled up in it,

…go to your PARACLETE, the Holy Spirit of Truth, living within you, go to Him immediately, the moment you realize what is happening to you, or what has happened to you,

…run to Jesus and His Spirit within you immediately, amen, and come back into <u>faith</u>,

…looking away from that sin, unto Jesus, the author and perfecter of our faith!

…the strengthener of our faith!

…the finisher of our faith!

…the One who makes it complete, who brings it to it's completion, who brings it back to <u>accuracy</u>, to it's proper <u>conclusion</u>,

…and He is also then the enforcer of our faith, amen; He reinforces it, He backs it up with power!

Thus, He is the One who reminds us of the truth, and brings us to maturity,

…to the maturity of what faith reveals,

And not only that, but as I already said: He enforces it with power in our lives!

...that's what maturity calls for: POWER; real power – the power to actually live this thing!

"Greater is He that is in us, than He that is in the world!"

"...I can do all things, through Christ, who strengthens me!"

"...and this is the victory that overcomes this world; that overcomes sin, even our faith!"

...and so you see, these scripture verses, these sayings **are not just mere empty cliche's any more.**

Listen the minute you become aware of the temptation, of that snare the enemy is trying to snare you in, *deal immediately with that thing, deal aggressively with it, and get away from it,*

...or better yet, don't just run away in weakness and in fear, being intimidated by that thing, stand up to it, and boldly confront it, and overcome it, and get rid of it, and get it out of your life!

Deal immediately with that thing and deal aggressively with that thing *and get it under your feet, where it belongs, and defeat it permanently, and get it out of your life, permanently!*

...get it out of your mind,

...because if you don't do it, if you keep entertaining Sin in your mind, that alternative identity; that idol, that lying image of yourself ...and yield to it,

...it will affect your authority, over sin,

...and over evil spirits,

...and it will affect your sense of righteousness,

...your enjoyment of your righteousness,

If you continue to entertain Sin in your mind and yield to sin in your spirit and in your life,

...it will affect your conscience,

...your consciousness of innocence and righteousness,

...it will affect your innocence consciousness,

...and it will then also affect your intimate fellowship with God,

..it is bound to, amen, you will not have any choice in the matter,

...it will affect your righteousness,

…your enjoyment of recognition before God,

If you continue to entertain Sin in your mind and yield to sin in your spirit and in your life,

…it will affect your authority, before God,

…it will affect that authority with God,

…and it will affect your anointing!

…it will affect the flow of authority and anointing!

…it will affect your ability to flow in it!

…you will no longer be able to flow in the anointing like you should!

*…like I said before, **that flow might even dry up all together!***

*…**so don't do it, amen!***

*…**don't keep messing with sin,***

*…**it's not you portion!***

*…**Sin is not your lot in life, nor is it your identity***

*…**it's not your identity!***

*…**so stop yielding to it!***

Chapter 11

Satan's Power Only Works Through Deception!

Hey listen, **the dominion that the Devil operates in, *functions only through deception!***

…it functions only through deception!

He is the father of lies!

I want us to quickly notice what it says there in 2 Corinthians 4:4,

"…in their case, the god of this world, has blinded the minds, of the unbelievers, to keep them, from seeing the light, of the gospel…"

"…that gospel, which has to do with the glory of Christ, who is the likeness of God."

The gospel has to do with His righteousness,

…**righteousness, by faith.**

That was exactly what the glory of Christ was all about.

It was about that righteousness, and authority,

…His righteousness, His authority,

…the righteousness He walked in, *by faith!*

But he says here,

"In the case of the unbelievers *(or even the ignorant believer, who does not understand these things),"*

He says,

"In their case, the god of this world has blinded their minds!"

The Devil is trying his best, to use this world and the mind-sets of this world; *their natural identity,*

"…to keep them from seeing, the light (or the truth), of the gospel"

Who does the god of this world have dominion over?

The ignorant ones, *and the unbelievers!*

Do you see that?

The ones who <u>do not</u> believe!

…who either do not believe, because they simply <u>do not know</u> these things,

...or they do not believe, because <u>they are ignoring it</u>, and therefore are also <u>being distracted</u> from it,

...or they are ignoring it, because of <u>a stubborn refusal to believe</u>!

...because they love darkness, more than light,

...because their deeds are evil, and they prefer it that way!

So, who does the Devil have dominion over?

Only those, who <u>do not know</u> the gospel and or <u>do not *believe*</u> the gospel!

"...the god of this world, has blinded the minds, of the unbelievers"

Now who exactly are the unbelievers?

Who are those who do not believe?

It is those who do not have a sensitive relationship to the word; *to the truth of the gospel.*

So Satan only has power if you walk in unbelief!

And what is unbelief?

Unbelief is the fruit of deception!

Unbelief is embracing a lie about oneself and about God!

Unbelief is seeing yourself *as less than* the way God sees you!

Unbelief is believing things about yourself *which God does not intimately know and therefore believes about you!*

Unbelief is *partaking of the tree of the knowledge of good and evil, instead of partaking of the tree of life!*

Unbelief is *coming in agreement with the image of yourself portrayed and projected by the Law of works, instead of coming in agreement with the Law of Faith and what that Law of perfect liberty reveals and declares about you!*

Unbelief is *the fruit of the Fall!*

Quickly also go with me to Ephesians 4, and we can see the same thing there.

Let's read from verse 17,

"Now this I affirm, and testify to in the Lord"

In other words, *I say the same thing as the Lord says about this!*

I bear witness to His truth in other words; *to His testimony concerning you!*

He says,

"I affirm, that you should no longer live as the gentiles do."

Who is he speaking to?

Christians

He says to them,

'Listen, believer, no longer live like the gentiles do.'

How do they live?

"They live in the futility of their minds;"

(The god of this world has an affect upon their minds)

"…they are darkened in their understanding!"

"They are alienated from the life of God!"

Why?

"Only because of, the ignorance, that is in them!"

Where did that ignorance come from?

"…it is due to their hardness of heart!"

Where did that come from?

Where did the hardness of heart come from?

Verse 19,

"They have become callous."

Where does that come from?

Where does callousness come from?

"They (no longer follow their true design speaking to them from within them, and) **have** (therefore) **given themselves up to licentiousness,** (where anything and everything goes, and nothing is off limits)."

"Therefore they are now greedy to practice every kind of uncleanness!"

That greediness comes from *a huge gaping hole in their heart; in their spirit!*

It is caused by spiritual starvation,

It comes from a deep seated gnawing hunger in their heart, in their spirit, that cannot be satisfied, by anything, *other than God Himself,*

...by anything other than their original, most authentic, true identity

...by anything other than righteousness,

...by anything other than intimate fellowship with God, embracing and

receiving His recognition, and approval, and affirmation, and applause of their life!

They are looking in the absolute wrong place for that **fulfillment!**

They are *led astray;* they are **blindfolded** *and* **going astray;** *wondering far away from the truth,*

...and looking *in the exact opposite place,* from where **real fulfillment; ultimate fulfillment** can be found!

So listen, then it is not God who is unjust, giving to some people favor, and others not!

God is not unjust in His dealings with Man!

God is not unjust!

They all have received favor!

Paul says, abundantly clearly, there in Ephesians 4:7,

"To each and every one of us, grace was given, according to the measure of Christ's gift!"

So, they all have received favor,

...but, if you give yourself up to uncleanness,

...if you give yourself up, to licentiousness,

...giving yourself a license to live by the flesh, to do whatever you want in your natural man; a license to sin, a license to live by the lust of the eyes, the lust of the flesh, and the pride of life,

...then your heart becomes callous, and hardened,

...and because of ignoring the truth and suppressing the truth in unrighteousness, <u>preferring</u> those other things; *this inferior alternative life, this inferior alternate lifestyle, <u>preferring it</u>* to a life lived in intimate relationship and fellowship and oneness with God, in the truth,

...then ignorance and darkness begin to reign again,

...and you begin to live by the course of this world again,

...and operate in the same mentality as they do again,

...the same mind, the same thinking, the same darkened understanding, *and deception,*

...following the prince of the power of the air again,

...following the sons of disobedience! ... and being a son of disobedience yourself ...ignoring and refusing to listen to the truth of the gospel!

Verse 20,

"BUT, you did not so learn Christ!"

"And I am assuming that you have heard about Him, and were taught in Him, (through the gospel; by the truth of the gospel, and by the Spirit of Truth Himself, through those who teach the gospel),"

...you were taught, according to the truth, as it is revealed, in Jesus!

"...and you were taught in Him, <u>as the truth is in Jesus</u>"

Then he says in verse 22,

*"**Therefore** (in the light of the truth, as it is revealed in Jesus) **put off that old nature,** (the old man, the old mentality and mindset, the one you embraced before, under the influence of the Fall, and of the Devil),"*

*"...**Put off the old mindset, that old mentality and its conduct, which belongs to, your former manner of life!**"*

"...your <u>former</u> manner of life!"

"…which grew __corrupt__, through __deceitful__ lusts, (distorted miss-placed passions and desires. Your former manner of life __grew more and more corrupt__ through strong unhealthy desires, that __appear__ good to you, but they __are not actually good__ for you!)"

Paul also writes the same thing to the Corinthians, and he challenged them in 1 Corinthians 3:3,

"Why are you acting, or behaving, like ordinary men?"

Listen, we are now free from the mentality of the flesh!

We no longer have an excuse, to be acting, or behaving, like ordinary men!

We __had__ a __former__ manner of life!

We need to receive that truth as fact!

We __had__ a former manner of life,

…before the truth of the gospel dawned on us,

…and we have to truly embrace that, *as a reality,* in our minds, and in our being,

…we need to thoroughly grasp that reality, and embrace that reality, *in our heart and in our spirit,* amen!

In 1 Peter 4:1-4, Peter also says the same thing!

"Since Christ suffered for us, in the flesh, (in our place, in a physical body that represented ours), *arm your mind, arm yourselves, with the same thought,* (with the same truth, with the same understanding, *with the law of identification, with the law of faith*), *for whoever <u>has suffered</u> in the flesh, has ceased from sin,"*

(...and we suffered there in Him, as He suffered as us, amen, so we have ceased from Sin, and we can now, therefore, cease from sin),

"...arm yourself, with the same thought, with the same mind, with the same truth, with the same faith,"

"...so as to live, for the rest of the time in the flesh, no longer, by human (inordinate, distorted) passions, but by the will of God."

And then he says, verse 3,

"Let the time that is past, suffice, for doing what the gentiles like to do!"

(...in other words, we have done what the gentiles do; what the unbelievers do, for long enough!)

"...they are living in licentious passions, and in drunkenness, reveling and

347

carousing, and living in spiritually lawless idolatry of themselves, and of others, and of the things in this word."

We had a former manner of life, *and there is a <u>new</u> manner of life now, revealed, and available, for us to live, and enjoy, in union with Christ Jesus!*

...a <u>new</u> manner of life, *which is a life according to our original design and true identity as children of God;*

...it is the result of our eternal righteousness *restored to us in full; to the max!*

Can you now see how righteousness, how our true spirit identity, and actual identity, restored to us, is the basis, of this <u>new</u> manner of life?

Righteousness is the basis, *of a practical walk of purity* in Christianity!

...daily walking in God,

...in righteousness,

...in Godliness,

...in God likeness!

...in our original design and real identity, as children of God; our true identity,

…and in intimate fellowship with God!

That's our <u>new</u> manner of life!

Hey, there really is only one environment in which every idea of Devil; every idea of demonic power *loses oxygen.*

I say again: **There is only one environment in which the Devil's influence is completely dissolves and comes to nothing:**

Colossians 3:1 See yourselves co-raised and co-seated with Christ! Now ponder with persuasion the consequence of your co-inclusion in Him. Relocate yourselves mentally! Engage your thoughts with Throne Room realities, where you are co-enthroned with Christ, by and at and as God's right hand, to share in and exercise His very executive authority.

3:2 Becoming affectionately acquainted with throne room thoughts will keep you from being distracted again by the earthly [soul ruled] realm.

The footnote reads: *("Set your minds upon the things that are above and not upon the things below!" - RSV. Whatever you may face in your daily lives, rather acquaint yourselves with the greater reality, than to get caught up in that which is happening as a distraction from it! Acquaint yourselves with the greater reality; with the things that are above! **Do not engage the energy of the things that are below!***

Also note Romans 1:18, where the Greek word, KATECHO – **to echo downwards,** *is used. To ECHO downwards is the opposite to the word, ANOCHE –* **to echo upwards,** *found in Romans 2:4 and 3:26. Also look at 2 Corinthians 4:18, "We are not keeping any score of what seems so obvious to the senses on the surface; it is fleeting and irrelevant;* **it is the unseen realm within us which has our full attention and captivates our gaze!"**

A renewed mind conquers the space in our hearts previously occupied by worthless pursuits and habits. *See the Author's notes on "Earthbound vs. Heavenly Dimension Realities" at the end of Revelation Chapter 16 in the Mirror Study Bible.)*

3:3 Your union with His death broke the association with that world; see yourselves located in a fortress where your life is hidden with Christ in God!

Footnote again: *("In that day [after my resurrection and ascension]* **you will know that I am in my father, and you in me and I in you."** *- John 14:20. Occupy your mind with this new order of life;* **you died when Jesus died;** *therefore,* **whatever defined you before defines you no more!** *Christ, in whom the fullness of deity dwells,* **most accurately defines you now,** *within that fullness unveiled! The word, "hidden" can also be translated, secret; the secret of your life [as well as the secret to it] is* **your union and absolute** *oneness with Christ in God! See Colossians 2:9,10.*

*"Risen, then, with Christ **you must lift your thoughts above** where Christ now sits at the right hand of God, **you must be heavenly minded; not earthly minded,** for you have undergone death, in His death, and **your life is hidden away now in safety, in the secret place, with Christ in God. Christ is your life, when he is manifest you are made manifest in glory."** - Knox Translation.)*

3:4 The ₁unveiling of Christ, as defining our lives, immediately implies that, what is evident in him, *is equally mirrored in you!* The exact life on exhibit in Christ is now *repeated in us.* We are included in the same bliss and joined-oneness with him; just as his life reveals <u>you</u>, *your life reveals <u>him</u>.*

Footnote: *(This verse was often translated to again delay the revelation of Christ to a future event, but the word, ₁OTAN, often translated as "when" is better translated as "**every time.**" Thus, "Every time Christ [who is our life] is revealed [out of us] we are being co-revealed in his glory." According to the Walter Bauer Lexicon, that Greek word, OTAN **is often used of an action that is repeated.***

*Paul reveals **our joint-glorification in Christ!** We are **co-revealed in the same bliss.** See 1*

Corinthians 2:7-8; Romans 3:23-24; Romans 8:30 and 2 Peter 1:3.

In him we live and move and have our being; in us he lives and moves and has his being! - *Acts 17:28.)* - Mirror Study Bible.

Chapter 12

Totally Persuaded!

Now all this that was said in this book, was said, **to help you become, fully established, in the reign of righteousness,**

...it was said, *so that you can realize* that, **the legal, and the practical result, of the gift of God's grace to you,** *which was demonstrated, in the person and in the death and resurrection of Jesus Christ,* **is given to you, and it is there,** *to put you into a much better position,* **than what Adam put you into!**

...*to put you into a much better position,* **than the average unenlightened Christian out there!**

God wants to put you into a much better position!

God wants to put you into a position, where the result of what Jesus revealed in His life and accomplished in His death and resurrection, *would much more powerfully affect your life,*

...than the result of Adam's sin!

God wants you to enjoy, *life more abundantly!*

...eternal life!

...victorious Christian living!

God wants you to be in a position, where the gift of His grace, and the revelation of righteousness, in your heart, *will be <u>out of all proportion</u>, to the effect of Adam's fall, and Satan's rule!*

...so that, not one of us, will walk in any excuse to sin; to adopt and live an inferior identity.

...God doesn't want us to settle for and live any inferior identity, aother identity, other than the original identity He gave us, amen!

...that's the only true authentic life there is; the original, amen!

I pray that this truth of your true identity and righteousness restored will gets so a hold of you, that you cannot help BUT live it! ...and man, you'll just begin to walk in the victory, with Jesus!

...and every opportunity to sin, that comes to you ...you'll just laugh at it,

...and rejoice in the fact, in the <u>reality</u> that, we are in dominion over Satan!

We are in dominion over his lies!

And we are not just in dominion over His lies, and His deception,

...to just preserve ourselves,

No, but we are out to conquer this globe together with God!

We are out to set the captives free!

We are out, through our ministry, to enforce the result of Jesus' resurrection!

That's what the ministry of the Gospel is all about!

The work of evangelism, and the great commission, is not merely some Christian doctrine, and some religious command, or obligation,

...some weak effort of man, in his own energy, to try and make some stand for God!

No, we proclaim God's <u>eternal truth</u>, *the truth of the gospel,* boldly, with confidence,

...knowing that it's the truth ...and knowing that the Devil does not stand a chance *against the truth;* against the power of the gospel, and against the power of God, *because God backs up His gospel with power*!

The ministry of reconciliation, the preaching and proclaiming of the gospel, the work of evangelism, *is the powerful effort of God ...through His Church; through us, each and every believer,*

...to reclaim lost property, to reclaim His kidnapped kids!

It's the powerful effort of God, through His Church, *to reclaim the lost ground,* amen!

It is like a little leaven that will keep spreading, until it has leavened the whole lump!

You see, under the Old Covenant, yeast, or leaven, was a picture of sin, *of how sin would have an initial introduction,* **but then it will also have a long term affect in someone's life, if it is entertained.**

And when Jesus spoke about His kingdom, His domain, His rule and reign of righteousness, *being just like leaven, leavening three measures of flour,*

...those three measures of flour, **measured out exactly, accurately,** were an indication that *it was going to have not only an initial impact and quick affect,*

*…but also that it was going to have a complete effect upon God's whole creation, because of **a complete affect upon the whole of mankind!***

Let me put it to you in another way.

When you decide to bake, and you have an unusually large amount of flour, *you can't just throw the leaven in there, and hope it will leaven all the flour.*

No, you have to use the right ratio.

You have to measure *accurately!*

That's why Jesus mentions three measures of flour.

It is not the three measures of flour that is the significant picture here,

…but it is the fact that there has been released, <u>an absolute sufficient measure</u> of leaven, of truth, <u>accurate truth</u>, to be able to leaven the whole lump, to leaven all the flour, that is what the significant picture is here!

If we measure the gospel <u>*accurately*</u>, then there will be a sufficient enough release of leaven, <u>of truth and power</u>, to leaven the whole lump, *to influence, and take back, all of humanity!*

Now with sin, *there was enough legal merit in Adam's transgression, for Satan to affect all of mankind with!*

But now, with the gospel, *the truth of the gospel is also just like that leaven,*

…it is just like Adam's transgression, *in its affect,*

…in fact, it is **<u>much greater</u>** in its affect, because it is *much more powerful,*

…*it is much more true!*

…*It is ultimate truth, amen!*

There is enough legal merit, in the gospel, to affect all of mankind with!

…That's what the gospel is like, if you were to try and *compare the gospel and its ability,* to Adam and to the Devil and their ability to affect mankind!

The leaven of the gospel, *will much more powerfully and thoroughly affect, all of mankind!*

Why do I say that?

I mean, *can we really believe that?*

Oh yes, we can, and **you had better believe it,**

...because, the disease of Sin spreads; the effects of it; *sin spreads, but it is not natural, it is against the true design of the human race*.

It is like an intruder, *like a virus that does not belong!*

Therefore the gospel, *the truth of the gospel, is much more powerful!*

...much more natural, to the design of the human race!

...and, therefore, it will catch on, much more quickly!

...and be much more powerful in its affect, and its effects!

...but only if it is measured accurately and presented properly!

So the picture of leaven, *is all about the fact that it affects an environment,*

And now that same picture is being used to describe *how Sin affected the whole world,*

...the effect of it is the disease of sin that is still spreading, but slowly, with resistance.

But how much more, *out of all proportions more effective,* it says, *will the truth of the gospel,* and therefore the kingdom of Jesus Christ, the government of Jesus, the reign and the rule, the authority of righteousness, *leaven and affect humanity,* and effect the world!

It will affect humanity and it will affect and impact the whole world!

It will much more, <u>out of all proportion</u> affect the whole world!

…and its effects will spread much quicker, <u>out of all proportion quicker</u>, than the effects of sin!

That's the picture!

Do you see that?

Just as Sin affected the whole world, and had its effect, *much more, <u>out of all proportions more</u>, will righteousness now affect the whole world, and have its effect upon it!*

I want you to see it clearly, because the Church as a whole, every single Christian, needs to get this message!

Because, Jesus says, God says,

"As surely as I live, all the earth shall be filled with <u>the (intimate) knowledge</u> of My glory, as the waters cover the sea, it shall be flooded with My Glory!"

…Like a tsunami wave!

...Flooded with <u>My</u> glory!

*...*And God's glory, is the fruit, of the reign of righteousness!

You see, the revelation of and embrace of that righteousness; *of your true identity fully restored to you,* immediately brings, God's glory, *to your spirit!*

The reign of righteousness is the only thing that can bring *God's glory* to your spirit,

...to anyone's spirit!

The reign of righteousness, is the only thing that can bring *the full manifestation* of God's glory, on the earth, permanently!

The glory of God *comes into manifestation,* when the reign of righteousness takes over!

What is the glory of God?

It is God's power and presence, yes,

*...*but it's also, the *'DOXA'* in the Greek, the opinion of God; *what God knows to be true about you!*

*...*what God knows to be <u>the truth</u> about you, according to His original design and identity that He gave you, and according to the truth of the successful work of reconciliation!

That is the glory!

What God <u>knows</u> to be <u>the truth</u> about you, *that is the glory, what it's all about, and it's the content, of the gospel!*

The glory of God comes immediately to my spirit, *when the truth of the gospel dawns on me,*

...when the revelation, and reign of righteousness, takes over,

It comes immediately, *through revelation;* through the revelation that I am declared righteous, and therefore made righteous, through what the blood of Jesus, demonstrates and reveals!

When I, *through that revelation, implement the law of identification; the law of faith,*

...when I implement that law of identification, that law of faith, through revelation,

...that's when the perfect Law of <u>liberty</u> sets in and takes charge!

...and therefore that's also when the glory of God is awakened in my spirit, and comes alive in my life!

...the glory of revelation knowledge!

...the glory of the faith of God!

…the glory of His joy!

…the glory of His peace!

…the glory of the knowledge of God!

That whole glory of God opens up to me!

…heaven itself, the very presence of God, the bosom of God, enjoying His measureless love, even the power of God, it all opens up for me!

…enjoying limitless fellowship, and intimacy and innocence in oneness with His Spirit opens up for me!

…that glory opens up to me!

…the glory of God opens up to me!

Oh hallelujah!

Can you see that!?

"All the earth shall be filled with My glory!"
- says God!

I am telling you, that is God's vision for His Church, and in fact for this whole world, and He has no plan B.

God's vision is the *effects* of holiness!

We cannot afford to settle for any vision less than that!

God's vision is to *affect* this whole world, with His gospel, and with His glory in us, revealed, in us, and through us!

God wants us to reclaim His lost property, His lost kids, His deceived kids; *His kidnapped kids,*

...with the truth of the gospel, and with all authority!

God wants us to reclaim the lost ground!

He says,

...the gates of hell; the gates of that hell Satan erected and built and established as his stronghold upon the earth, through the Fall ...the <u>gates</u> of that hell; *that which fortifies and strengthens that hell,* <u>shall not prevail</u> against His Church!

That's what Jesus said!

"I will build My Church and the gates of Hell shall not prevail against My Church!"

...because we are going to bust those gates down, amen!

...we are going to break through in people's thinking; we are going to tear those strongholds of lies and deception down!

...we are going to set the captives free!

...we are going to bring them in,

...because the gift of God's grace has much more powerfully affected the human race,

...and that gift of God's grace in us, that righteousness, that authority, is therefore now, out of all proportion, to the power of sin, and the power of the Devil, to keep mankind bound, amen!

Of the increase of Jesus' rule and reign, of God's government, *through His Church,* there shall be no end!

I do not believe that God's vision for this book I am writing, or for my life and ministry, for the churches and discipleship schools I am involved with, (and for even the church you are a part of) ...**God's vision for us *is not,* to barely have an impact; *an insignificant impact!***

I believe that God's vision for our ministry, for the ministry of reconciliation, for the ministry of Jesus, for the ministry of the true gospel of grace, is, *to affect the utter most parts of the earth!*

I am totally convinced of this!

And I am totally convinced that, at least as far as my life and ministry is concerned, *that this will happen,*

...because I am not prepared to identify and acknowledge and approve of any ministry among us, or in the world,

...any ministry that I am involved with,

...I am not prepared to identify with, and approve of that ministry any more, *if it does not line up with God's vision!*

God has entrusted us, with the right measure, with the right ingredients, to put it into the flour, *and to leaven the whole lump with it!*

He has entrusted us, with the right gospel, and there is enough in that gospel, enough truth, enough authority, enough power,

...there is enough of an active ingredient, in the leaven of God's gospel, *to affect our whole environment,*

...and this whole world also!

I am telling you, there is enough legal, and vital, and practical and real authority, and truth integrity and power, in this message, in the message of the gospel; *in the ultimate truth revealed in Jesus and proclaimed in the gospel,*

...to affect our whole nation,

...to affect all the nations of the world,

…every nation,

…even the communist ones,

…and the nations, like China, that follow Confucius,

…and the Hindu nations,

…and even the Muslim nations!

…_even_ the Muslim nations!

They are our inheritance, amen!

They are our brothers and sisters, _and they are merely deceived and confused you see,_ but they are our brothers and sisters none the less, _and they need rescuing, just like we all once did;_ they are our inheritance to claim, our portion; _our most immediate and dear family members!_

I am convinced that the gospel of God will not stay, within the limits of this book,

…_or within the limits of the church,_

…_or within the limits of any discipleship school,_

…_or within the limits of our hearts, for that matter!_

…_or even within the limits of your heart either!_

I am convinced that this is a message which time has come!

I am convinced that it will break forth!

I am convinced that it will multiply!

I am convinced that the word of God, that the truth of the gospel, produces!

I am convinced it produces after its own kind!

I am convinced that it will bear fruit!

And I am convinced that that fruit will reach the utter most parts of the earth!

I am convinced that God's word of truth, the gospel of our salvation in Christ Jesus, will reach the utter most parts of the earth!

I am convinced that if you drink of this water, it will become within you a fountain of life!

…an artesian well that never will run dry,

…even rivers of living water, shall gush forth out of my inner-most being, and out of your inner-most being!

I am absolutely convinced of it, because Jesus Himself said so!

I am sold on God's Seed principle and God's principle of multiplication!

I am convinced that even through this book, God Himself is equipping you!

I am convinced that He is making us, through an accurate understanding and revelation into the gospel; into the truth of the gospel, *He is making us competent ministers, not of the Old Covenant, no, but of the New Covenant; the ultimate Covenant, the original Covenant restored!*

I am totally convinced that as you muse, and ponder, on what was said here in this book, *that rivers of living water will issue forth from your inner most being!*

I am totally convinced that your whole world will know about it!

Ha... ha... ha...

Hallelujah!

I am totally convinced that the whole world will hear about the success of the cross; *of what was so clearly revealed and accurately displayed by God in it!*

...they will hear and know about the grace of God,

...and about what that grace successfully revealed and accomplished, on our behalf, and their behalf!

I am totally convinced, because I know the integrity that has been invested in this gospel!

I am totally convinced, because I know what is in this gospel!

...I know that the gift of God's grace, is out of all proportion, to Adam's wrong doing!

...to Satan's power!

I know that it is *out of all proportion,* to Adam's and Satan's deal, that they had going, there in the Garden!

It is *out of all proportion!*

It's *much* larger!

It's *much* bigger!

It's *much* better!

It's *much more powerful,* amen!

Hey, let's not insult God, and say to Him,

'God, Your gospel is but a weak effort!'

Listen, it's the strongest effort that God could ever produce!

He has revealed His arm!

He has revealed His strength, in His Son, *in this gospel!*

...and He says, "...the nations will <u>see</u> it!"

Hallelujah!

The gospel <u>*is*</u> the power of God!

God's power *is directly attached* to the gospel!

His integrity is behind the gospel!

He backs it up *with power,* amen!

There is *enough power* in the gospel!

It is *out of all proportions powerful!*

Ha... ha... ha...

Hallelujah!

It is *out of all proportions powerful!*

...Just as much as light is *out of all proportions, more powerful,* than darkness!

It takes just one little match, *to bring light,* to a whole room full of darkness!

The minute you turn on the light, *darkness flees,* amen!

Ha… ha… ha…

Hallelujah!

When the light comes, *darkness has to go!*

It has to go, amen!

It has no choice!

The gospel is *much more powerful,* than all the forces of darkness, combined!

I am convinced of it!

If we preach, *the right gospel,* we will see the right results!

I am convinced of it!

And that's why, I, for myself, I will never again *settle for the lie of the Devil, emphasized in that other gospel; the man-made gospel; the gospel of man's efforts dependent on man's performance!*

Hey, the Devil, and his gospel which religion promotes, *is fighting a losing battle, against God, and against the real gospel,*

…against <u>the truth</u> of that gospel!

You shall know the truth, *and the truth shall make you free; completely free,* amen!

I am telling you; there is enough truth in the gospel, *to set this whole world free!*

There might be a terrific battle ahead of us, Church, against religion, and legalism, *for the hearts and minds of people*

...but there is going to be *great victory upon victory, upon victory!*

...until the Devil, and his message, is *utterly defeated!*

...until all God's enemies *are made His footstool!*

...Because people are designed for the gospel, *they are custom designed for the truth of the gospel,* and the Holy Spirit of truth will bear strong witness with their spirits that they are indeed the children of God, designed and brought forth to give expression, exclusively so, to His image and likeness, *engraved upon their inner-man!*

We are in the most exciting business there could possibly be man, I'm telling you!

...Because, what we proclaim and produce, *those fruits of righteousness has a definite impact!*

...it has an impact!

...And it multiplies!

Ha... ha... ha...

Amen!

Hallelujah!

Many think that religion is all about God, but for God, *it's all about people!*

Do you really want to love God, *more?*

Then love others the same way that you are supposed to love yourself.

An accurate love for oneself and for others can only happen in the revelation of what God Himself revealed about us in the gospel; *our true value and worth; our true identity!*

You see, the lost coin in Luke 15 *never lost its original value!*

Therefore, ***"Speak evil of no-one,"*** says Paul to Titus; ***"show perfect courtesy towards everyone – for we ourselves were once ignorant!"*** he says. - Titus 3:2-4.

Hey, I say again: **Neither the lost coin, not the lost sheep, nor the lost son, *ever lost their original value!***

The fact that the treasure was hidden from view, *didn't diminish its authentic worth!* No, the man (Jesus; God the Father – the entire Godhead) who came and redeemed the

374

hidden treasure there in Matthew 13:44, **sold all He had,** *to buy the entire field!*

I can't remember if I have said this before, here in this book, but let me end with these thoughts:

You see, Jesus' shed blood was not to buy us back from the Devil; *a thief never gets ownership!* - Psalm 24:1. **Neither was it to persuade His Father to forgive us –** *it was to persuade our minds of God's eternal esteem of us,* **and thus free us from the lies that we believed about ourselves!** - Hebrews 6:16-17.

My friend Francois Du Toit often says, **"People are not born Christians,** *yet every person ever born comes from God!*

God says in Jeremiah 1:5 *"I knew you before I formed you in your mother's womb!"*

We are God's idea: *we began in God!*

We are born into a world where we are bombarded with many diverse cultural and traditional mindsets, most of which directly stems from the Tree of the knowledge of good and evil system, *which is the fallen mindset system which says* **you are not** *...***you have to strive to become!**

People who do gross things *do it* **from believing a lie about themselves, and from** *not knowing the truth of their incredible design as image bearers of God!*

James says in James 3:9,

*"We can say beautiful things about God the Father **but with the same mouth curse a man <u>made in his mirror likeness</u>."***

*"...**These things aught not to be so!**"* he says.

You see, the point is not *what the man did to deserve the curse!* The point is *we are all made in God's mirror likeness **and need constant reminders of that truth and reality, rather that having curses pronounced over us, which reinforce the lies and the Devil's stronghold in people's hearts and minds!***

As I said before: A doctor doesn't slap his patient and command him to stop coughing! **You may have the flu, *but you never become the flu!***

True worship is **to touch someone's life with the same devotion and care you would touch Jesus himself; *even if the other person seems a most unlikely candidate.***

Multitudes of people are living in the darkness of ignorance, **not knowing the truth of the integrity of their design and their redeemed value and innocence!**

...Therefore the adventure of the Christian life is **to declare,** *what we have discovered to be true,* **about every single person!**

Jesus says that **when we discover that the son of man is indeed the son of God,** *then, and then only, the gates of Hell; the gates of HADES (not to see) will crumble, and the prisoners of darkness will be free, to discover themselves in him!*

In closing, I urge you to get yourself a copy of *"The Mirror Study Bible,"* it is the best paraphrase translation of the Scriptures from the original Greek that I have ever read, and it's available online at: www.amazon.com and Barnes & Noble, and several other book sellers.

If you want me or someone a part of our team to come to where you are, *anywhere in the world,* and give a talk or teach you and some of your friends *about the gospel message and these redemption realities,* simply contact us at www.livingwordintl.com ...or you can always find me on www.facebook.com

If your life has changed as a result of reading this book, *please write to me and let me know.*

I would love to share in your joy,

...so that my joy in writing this book may be full!

"That which was from the beginning,

which we have heard
(**with our spiritual ears**),
which we have seen
(**with our spiritual eyes**),
which we have looked upon
(**beheld, focused our attention upon**),
and which our hands have also handled
(**which we have also experienced**),

concerning the Word of life,

379

we declare to you,

that you also may have this
fellowship with us;

and truly our fellowship is with
the Father
and with His Son Jesus Christ.

And these things we write to you
that your joy may be full."

- 1 John 1:1-4

About the Author

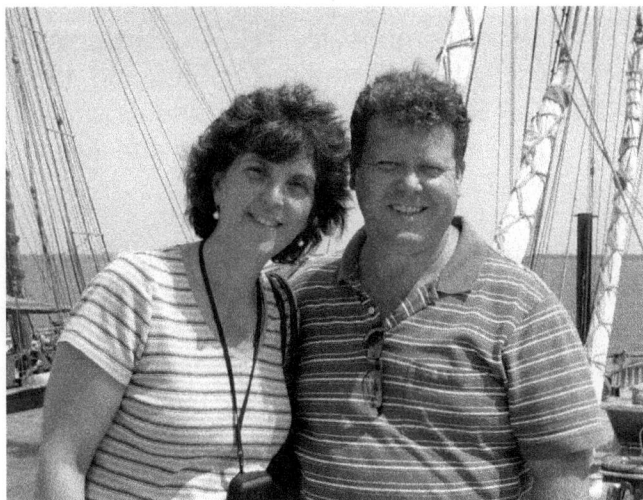

Rudi & Carmen Louw together oversee: Living Word International, which is what they named their ministry, **because, they love to travel and minister both locally and internationally.**

Rudi was born and raised in the country of South Africa, while Carmen grew up in Cortland, New York.

They function in the ministry of reconciliation (2 Corinthians 5:18-21) and flow strongly with the Holy Spirit and His anointing to teach, preach, prophesy, heal, and whatever is needed to touch people's lives with the reality of God's love and power.

God has given them keen insight into what He has to say to mankind in the work of redemption *concerning the revelation and restoration of humanity's true identity.*

Therefore they emphasize THE GOSPEL, IN CHRIST REALITIES, the GRACE of God, the WORD OF RIGHTEOUSNESS, *and all such eternal truths essential to salvation and living the CHRIST-LIFE.*

They have been granted this wisdom and revelation into the knowledge of God by the resurrected Spirit of Jesus Christ, *to establish and strengthen believers in the faith of God, and to activate them in ministering to others.*

Not only are people set free from the poison and bondage of sin, condemnation and all kinds of intimidation, (upheld, strengthened and reinforced by age old religious ideas born out of ignorance) **but many are brought into a closer more intimate relationship with Father God, as Daddy**, through accurate teaching and unveiling of the gospel message, prophetic words, healings and miracles.

Rudi & Carmen are closely knitted together with many other effective Christians, church fellowships, and groups of believers who share the same revelation and passion **to impart the truth of the gospel to others, so as to impact and transform the world we live in with the LOVE and POWER of God.**